D0392477

LEADING WITH YOUR LEGACY IN MIND

LEADING WITH YOUR LEGACY IN MIND

Building Lasting Value in Business and Life

ANDREW THORN

New York Chicago San Francisco Athens London Madrid
Mexico City Milan New Delhi Singapore Sydney Toronto

2 3 4 5 6 7 8 9 0   DOC/DOC   1 2 0 9 8 7 6 5 4

ISBN   978-0-07-182984-7
MHID 0-07-182984-9

e-ISBN   978-0-07-182983-0
e-MHID 0-07-182983-0

McGraw-Hill Education books are available at special quantity discounts to use as premiums and sales promotions or for use in corporate training programs. To contact a representative, please visit the Contact Us pages at www.mhprofessional.com.

As a boy, I learned to work hard and dream big.

Thanks to you, Roger and Marylyn Thorn, for keeping me safe and allowing me to grow. Your legacy burns brightly inside of me.

Contents

PART I

The Roots of Leadership Legacy

PART II

The Arc of Leadership

PART III

The Seasons of Leadership

Foreword

Imagine that you are 95 years old and just getting ready to die. Here comes your last breath! Just before you take that breath, you are given a beautiful gift: the ability to go back in time and talk to the person who is reading this foreword. What advice would the 95-year-old you, who knows what really mattered in life and what did not matter, have for the you that is here today?

In terms of creating your legacy, that will be the only thing that matters. If that old person says that you did the right thing, you did. If that old person says that you made a mistake, you did. You don't have to impress anyone else.

Leading with Your Legacy in Mind will help to ensure that the you who will one day be facing death will be proud of the you who lived your life. Your actions are what create that confidence. Nothing could be more important.

Andrew Thorn is a friend and my personal coach. He taught me the wonderful "daily question" process that I have been using for years. He has helped me keep what really matters in my life in focus.

Andrew is a dedicated man who is sincerely and authentically making a positive difference for his friends, his family, and the world.

My suggestion is that you read *Leading with Your Legacy in Mind* very slowly. Think about what each chapter means for you and your life.

Please take the time to reflect upon how you can build lasting value in your business and in your life.

The great ideas in this book will help you only if you apply them in your life. Our greatest challenge isn't understanding the practice of leadership—it is practicing our understanding of leadership.

Andrew Thorn has helped me have a better life, both at work and at home. He can do the same for you. If you are open to the ideas in this book and put them into practice, you will live a legacy that will extend well beyond your lifespan.

Life is good!

MARSHALL GOLDSMITH

Preface

The wheels are up, and my plane is flying homeward through the night. Buenos Aires is now five hours behind me, and I find myself somewhere over the coast of Peru. It is a moment of celebration. This week, I successfully launched a project that will significantly enhance the revenues of our firm and provide us with an amazing opportunity to strengthen and shape the growth and culture of our global brand.

It was a long workweek, and I am tired, but the opportunity to do what I do best within the walls of an amazing organization makes my 22-hour trek home from my client's office pass quickly. My excitement makes this beast of a commute bearable, but that doesn't change the fact that I will spend more nights this week in seat 2A than I will in my own bed. I have been away for only a week, and yet it seems like an eternity. I am anxious to get home, but I am worried that when I get there, I won't have enough energy to be the loving husband and the caring father that I so want to be.

As these thoughts push their way into my consciousness, a conflict that I know all too well begins to rage between my head and my heart. It is an argument that many of us face without ever finding a real resolution.

On the one hand, I argue, "This is how I make a living. This is how I am valued in the world. This is how I provide a good life for my family.

This is what I am meant to be doing. Don't I deserve to be successfully engaged in the work that I love so much? Don't I deserve to be recognized as an expert in my field? Isn't this what I have worked so hard to do over the last many years? Isn't this me, living into my purpose? If not now, then when will I be able to do what I am meant to do?"

Then the side of me that represents what I value most begins to make the counterargument. "There is no long-term meaning for me in this project. This is taking me away from my family. This opportunity will cause me to miss so many beautiful moments—you know, the moments that I always say are so important. What good is the life that I am providing for my family if I am not there to enjoy it with them? Is this really worth it? How will I be able to balance my life and my work commitments? How will I stay connected to a deeper purpose? How will I find meaning when I will be spending so many nights in a hotel room all by myself each month? How can I do this to myself again?"

The excitement and frustration spark endless rounds of debate. I am too exhausted to sleep, so I stare out the window, watching the moonlight reflected on the dark Pacific Ocean below. I will arrive in Los Angeles at 12:30 a.m. By the time I clear customs and make the long drive home from the airport, it will be just past 3:00 a.m. when I finally crawl into bed next to the woman I love. My children will be excited to see me, so they will wake me up early with hugs and kisses so that we can catch up while they anxiously wait for a fun day with their dad. I can't wait to be there, but I can wait to be there.

The mindless roaming of my thoughts suddenly shifts, and I realize that the idea that I can ever obtain a true balance between my personal and professional responsibilities is a monstrous myth. The conflict between my work and my life will always exist. The answer is not one or the other. I will always need both if I am to feel like a total person. I will always need both if I am to feel whole. I deserve to learn and to grow; after all, that is why I am here. There will always be an inequality in the amount of time I spend in each of these two domains. Any work that I might do would require a similar sacrifice.

Whether I like it or not, I must work. It is an essential part of creating a happy life. Without it, I would be unable to fund a peaceful existence. The question is not, "Why must I leave behind what I value most so that I can give the majority of my attention to what I know matters least?" but rather, "How can I use the time that I have effectively in both of these domains so that I am more than just a survivor? How do I thrive in the ever-churning mix of quantity and quality?"

As I ponder these questions, I realize just how difficult it is to satisfy the demands of these competing influences. This struggle brings to light an amazing conflict. Part of me needs and wants to be home with my family, while another part of me wants and needs to be out making my mark in the world. I realize that either one without the other would lead to a breakdown of catastrophic proportions. I need both, but satisfying both seems impossible. As I evaluate and reevaluate my journey, I realize that my legacy depends upon my ability to successfully discover the right amount of focus to place on each of these critical areas. Being home all the time would prevent me from satisfying my need to create, but being away all the time would destroy the bloom of my most beautiful creations.

Perhaps you have felt the same way. Maybe you don't have to travel as far I do to get to your job, but I am sure that your work is just as consuming as mine. I imagine that there are many nights when you arrive home with nothing left to give, and, like me, you find yourself wondering, is this the way it has to be? Is the constant sacrifice of what I value most required if I am to have the professional experiences that help me to learn, to grow, and to develop?

We spend most of our lives trying to figure out the answers to these questions. We want to spend the time we have wisely, so we search for a way to strike a balance between our lives and our leadership passions. We reach for our legacy with a tremendous amount of uncertainty. We hope for meaning, while we labor each day for money.

I hope this book will help you in your leadership journey.

Acknowledgments

There are many people who have directly and indirectly influenced the writing of this book. They were either here long before I began, or there to support me along the way. I wish to acknowledge your help. Though I can't mention all of you by name, you know when and how you have contributed and you will recognize your influence in my writing. There are some, however, whom I must single out.

To McGraw-Hill: Thank you for believing in me and in this work.

To Marshall Goldsmith: You believed in me and allowed me to contribute to your success. Your invitation to help put me in position to do great work.

To Tom Miller (executive editor) and John Willig (agent): Whether you both know it or not, you became the driving forces behind this effort, which caused me to expand both my vision and my purpose. This book would never have happened without both of you.

To Jack Zanger: You always make time for me. Thank you for being the model of an Extraordinary Leader.

To Kurt Anderson, Maxim Allan Williams, and Don Grayson: You were all there in the beginning. Your help was significant in fanning the flames in my soul.

To Eddie Peterson: You helped me to see myself on a higher plane and gave me an opportunity to live in a divine moment.

To my editors Pattie Amoroso, Alice Manning, and Dannalie Diaz: Your fine-tuning and careful polishing created a new level of awareness in me that I won't soon forget. I am a better writer because of you.

Special thanks to Marylyn Thorn, Dave Bradley, Jill Barger, Carol Leonti, Eduardo Cortes, Rex McGuire, Bob Little, Sharon Sides, Robert Sarkissian, Mike Noll, Dana Triester, Christian Hart, Peter Child, Chuck Thorn, Wayne Strom, Andrea Molberg, Richard Wirthlin, David Feinberg, and Kashif Zubair: Your contributions are many and extremely evident throughout this book. Your love and support made it possible!

To my children, Scott, Christina, Jacob, Jacquelyn, Joseph, John, Sarah, Rebekah, and Leah: Because of you, I aspsire to lead and live with my legacy in mind. I love you so much.

Finally, to my wife, Stacy: This is a manifestation of your constant support and encouragement. I would not be who I am without your love. I love growing whole with you. I see you.

Introduction: Leadership and Legacy

There is a problem associated with the word *legacy*. While it generally inspires us to think big thoughts, it rarely inspires us to take action until it is too late. Why? Because we are busy, and we believe that we will eventually arrive at a place in life that will be less complicated and more conducive to working on our legacy.

Many of us, especially readers of this book, have imagined the theoretical aspects of legacy making. This book helps you to take action by confronting a different problem: leading with your legacy in mind. The difficulty of this problem is enhanced by the fact that most people today expect to be given a prescription for "how to create a legacy." You know, something simple that we can do in our free time; something that won't be too difficult or require us to think too much. I am afraid that anyone who approaches this book with this hope will be disappointed.

Leading with your legacy in mind requires work. To read this book correctly, you must be willing to enter the dimension that only you can control: the space inside your heart and mind. You must be willing to think about things, without the noise that so easily disturbs our thinking. You will need to let the things in this book hang around in your mind for a while—not because they are so profound or complicated, but because the answers must come from you, and it may take you a while to filter out the messages of the crowd so that you can hear the messages that come from inside you. Do not be afraid to engage. If fear is not your problem, then don't let your wonderful abilities to creatively avoid the things that matter most influence you any longer.

We are never too young to focus on our legacy-making efforts. In fact, the earlier you begin, the more meaning you will create. You must become a creator of circumstance, and not just a casual observer to your quickly passing life and career.

The guidelines in this book will help you understand how to create a legacy that will be much more than the financial wealth you accumulate and the high marks of your most significant achievements. They are presented in the form of continuums and arcs and are represented by the seasons of following, leading, and serving.

When you read this book, you will benefit from the development of three important practices.

First, legacy making requires discipline. I am not speaking of the kind of discipline that requires us to spend a certain amount of time each day, but rather the kind that keeps our legacy-making efforts in mind throughout all of our life and work experiences.

Specifically, this book is focused on discovering how to get the most out of your work. If you approach your work experiences with the thought that you are being forced to work for eight hours a day for purposes that are not your own and in ways that do not support you, your energy will be drained, and you will have very little time to think about your legacy. But if you allow yourself to become a personal best leader at work by taking charge of your career contributions, you will discover a rhythm in your work that will lead you to the realization of greater levels of purpose and meaning. The only way for you to get there is by being disciplined enough to think and act now.

Second, your legacy-making efforts will require you to develop new levels of concentration. Too often, we are easily distracted, and this causes us to run off chasing meaningless goals. The markers of our legacy are significant but subtle. When we couple this subtlety with the fact that the act of concentration is rare in our culture, we begin to understand why it is so difficult for us to discover the milestones of our own legacy. Leading with your legacy in mind requires you to sit still, in your own company, without any outside noise. Many people find this impossible. They become nervous and fidgety, and they give up before they even get started. You must be willing to concentrate.

Finally, you must be willing to develop patience, as it too is a necessary quality for your legacy-making efforts. It is important to note that nearly everything we are taught at work fosters the exact opposite. We want it done as quickly as it can possibly be done, and the quicker the better. Of course, there are many important economic reasons for this, but your legacy is not an economic proposition.

Leading with your legacy in mind is the most important work of your lifetime. You cannot hurry it up. Instead, you must be patiently engaged in this work each and every day.

As you develop greater levels of discipline, concentration, and patience, you will begin to see the real purpose and meaning of your life. You are here to learn and grow from your own experiences, and your time at work creates the laboratory for making that happen.

This book brings to life the *inventure* (the journey that goes on inside of you) that leads to your legacy. It highlights the legacy arcs and seasons that will help you in your personal efforts to build lasting value in your business, and in your life.

The journey begins by practicing discipline, concentration, and patience. The rewards are a life well spent, a meaningful career, a focus on making things better for others, and a legacy that demonstrates the differences you have made.

LEADING WITH YOUR LEGACY IN MIND

The Roots of Leadership Legacy

Chapter 1

Life + Leadership = Legacy

No man is born into the world whose work is not born with
him. There is always work.

—JAMES RUSSELL LOWELL

When we examine the equation that derives our legacy, we discover
that there are two primary variables: life and leadership.

The life subset includes anything and everything that fosters our
personal growth and development. Most of these experiences are quali-
tative, meaning that they are measured by how they make us feel. Our
health and our wellness are the key indicators of our success in this area.
It is in this domain that we discover who we are and dream about who
we want to become.

This is the part of the equation that brings vibrant color to our life.
This is where we are able to pursue our individual wants and needs. This
is how we define our values. A healthy legacy requires each of us to take
action in this area. In every case, we are responsible for living the life

that we want to live. No one can do it for us, but the busyness of the world makes it easy for us to forget that we are ultimately responsible for our quality of life.

Normally, the impact of our life experiences on our legacy is felt only within us. These internal indicators are difficult for others to value. There are external signs, but they are difficult for others to comprehend. These experiences are what make us unique. Our life contributions are made on our behalf and on behalf of those we love.

The leadership subset includes all our work experiences. Our skills, our knowledge, and our abilities contribute to the way in which our professional impact is felt by others. This is where we spend the majority of our time, and this is how we finance the quality of life that we seek. A healthy legacy requires us to feel good about the work we are doing. Sometimes our willingness to enter into employment contracts is based solely on the fact that we will be nicely compensated for our efforts. While the exchange of time for money is critical, we must be careful about agreeing to do work that fails to contribute to our sense of purpose and meaning.

Our leadership responsibilities often consume us. This is because we spend so much of our time dealing with them. Whereas our life responsibilities represent the qualities that we desire in life, our leadership responsibilities represent most of the quantities that we seek. Naturally, in order to establish our leadership identity, we must develop both competencies and behaviors. However, this identity is heavily influenced and defined by what we do. A failure on our part to develop ourselves personally may ultimately derail our efforts, but we all know people who are promoted and appreciated solely on the basis of what they do. As long as they can deliver a desired outcome, they are valued by the organization.

The key indicator of success in the leadership subset is achievement. We derive a lot of meaning from the stuff we are able to acquire as a result of our efforts, especially early in our lives. The more successful we are, the more things we have that demonstrate this success. There is generally a significant correlation between our work-related success and the prices of the house we live in, the car we drive, and the clothes we wear. Naturally, it is easy to believe that this correlation can be explained by the fact that since we are making more money, we can afford nicer things, but such an explanation fails to take into account the pressure we feel to showcase our success through our many acquisitions. After all, these acquisitions make it easier for us to demonstrate that we are successful.

I say this with an understanding that what I am stating is quite obvious, yet I feel that it is important to say it very clearly as we begin this journey together. Simply put, the two important variables of the legacy equation represent the qualities and the quantities that we experience during a lifetime. If we stay focused on the things that really matter, then our accumulated experiences can be additive and sometimes they can even be multiplicative. Sadly, when we lose our focus, or train our attention too much on one or the other, they can become subtractive and even divisive.

Much has been written about how we can learn to balance these subsets, but that is both unnecessary and impossible.

It is unnecessary because both subsets are located on the same side of the equation. Balance between these two important subsets was never meant to exist. Together, they make up the whole that we are seeking on the other side of the equation—our legacy. They are variables, which means that we will almost always have more of one than the other.

It is impossible to strike a balance because these two variables are very different from each other. Discovering how to measure a quality can be quite puzzling, while the measures of a quantity are easy for us to comprehend. When we are focused on finding a balance, we do our best to convert the qualities we desire into quantities. This is impossible to do. The qualities we enjoy will always be measured very differently from the quantities we amass, and it is meant to be that way.

Naturally, as we pursue meaning in our life and leadership responsibilities, we will spend unequal amounts of time in the two areas. In fact, most of our time during any 24-hour period is spent either making a living, taking care of our personal responsibilities, or sleeping. This leaves us with what feels like only a few precious moments each day to make meaning, and most of the time we are too exhausted to take advantage of them.

The answer lies not in finding a balance, but rather in creating a focus that amplifies our efforts in both of these areas. Most self-help books are written as a reminder to focus on the qualities, and many are written to encourage us to spend more time on the life elements of the equation. This is precisely why very few people benefit from the millions of words that are written each year. The advice we receive is too difficult for us to follow. The pressing demands of work are always there. They can never be abandoned.

Leadership Defined

It should be noted that nothing that I have written here is meant to be critical of the self-help literature. I truly believe that the time we spend in the pursuit of personal growth and development is time well spent. However, the focus of this book is on accepting the reality that we spend more time each day on our work-related responsibilities than we are able to spend on our life-related responsibilities. I say that we must accept this fact, because when we do, we become more capable of making sure that we are focused on doing the things that will allow us to create the most meaning in both our personal and professional domains.

Our focus now turns solely to our work-related roles and the responsibilities that each of us must carry out each day. Our purpose is to discover how to make the most of the time we must spend at work every day in the pursuit of providing for our personal needs.

To begin this conversation, we must be clear about what it means to be a leader. Our leadership opportunities are found within the realm of our work-related responsibilities. You and I are responsible for the development of the critical competencies that are associated with our professional roles and the leadership behaviors that we will need if we are to be promoted to greater responsibilities within the organizations where we work.

Sadly, leadership is generally established and defined by the title, the position, or the authority that a person is granted within the boundaries of an organizational structure. It is true that this establishes position power within the leadership chart, but it does nothing to establish a person's leadership capacity, or the acceptance of that person's leadership efforts by others.

Plain and simple, being a leader must always be about making things better for others, regardless of a person's formal role. Until you and I can do that, the position or title we hold is of little consequence.

The Leader, with a capital "L," is an important organizational agent, but this book is not about establishing title or position. Instead, it is about making sure that each of us is constantly engaged in the act of becoming a personal best leader, regardless of whether we find ourselves in a followership role, a leadership role, or even the role of a volunteer servant. No one needs a title to do that. Everyone can make things better for others, no matter where he or she is found on the organizational chart.

Small "l" leaders are everywhere, and our society needs more of them to stand up and be counted. More important, this is precisely the type of leadership that is required if we are to create and live into our legacy. The pursuit of roles and titles often blinds us to what really matters in our work experiences, but when we simply engage in making things better for others, our legacy emerges in a powerful way.

Jill's Leadership Story

The best way to illustrate this point is through the story of some work that I was privileged to do with Jill. She had a 35-year career at a municipality in the Pacific Northwest. She began in an entry-level position, and over the course of her career she worked in nearly every division of her organization without ever being appointed to a formal leadership role.

I was hired by her organization to facilitate a significant redesign of one of its key divisions. My scope included the creation of a new strategic vision and operating plan, a new reporting structure, the right-sizing of the organizational chart, and leadership coaching for the members of the new leadership team that emerged as a result of all these changes.

At the time, Jill was a member of the organization's change management team, and she was assigned to help me create and implement the desired transformation. Our work scared a lot of people. This particular municipality had historically had a low turnover rate, and it was known that quite a few people would be asked to move on. Many of the people who would be affected by our efforts had been with the organization for a very long time.

Despite the fact that Jill had never been a capital "L" leader, she was accepted throughout the organization as a person who had an extremely high amount of integrity. Everywhere we went, she opened the doors to change. Despite the intense nature of our assignment, and the fact that some of the senior leaders would be without a job when we were finished, we were able to get the buy-in we needed to make the project a success. Jill made this possible. Her authentic approach made it possible for us to engage in many difficult but productive conversations. Her internal credibility made my success on the job possible. Everyone knew her to be fair. Her knowledge of the organization made it possible for us to engage even those who would eventually be leaving in a productive way.

She made it possible for each affected person to contribute value in the creation of the new plan. This meant that those who left the company did so with their legacy intact. For years, it had been difficult to get people to retire or resign from their positions, and the municipality had suffered from this, but in this case many people left for their own good and for the good of the organization. Jill's informal leadership made it possible for us to lead them in this direction.

A few years after we finished the project, Jill herself retired from the organization. The company always celebrated the careers of its retirees by throwing them a going away party. Prominent leaders could expect a large turnout when they left. Jill's party was a minor affair. Only a few of the current employees attended her soirée, but many of the people she had worked with over the years sent notes of congratulations for a job well done. Jill left, and the organization moved on. Her legacy is found deep in the current structure of the organization, even though she never served it in anything more than what many would consider to be minor capacities.

This is the way it is for all of us, no matter what position we hold. We lead for a time and a season, and then someone else takes over. This is why it is so important for us to always remember to lead with our legacy in mind.

One day the responsibilities we currently hold will belong to someone else. That person will take over our professional role, but our legacy will remain and continue on with us. It is important that we learn how to get the most out of the 117,000 projected hours that we will spend on average over the course of our careers. Naturally, these hours will be focused on creating an outcome for the companies that employ us, but they must also be focused on creating the best possible personal legacy. If we want to make our mark, we must be conscious of our individual responsibility to get this done. Anything short of that will lead us only to a long and miserable work experience. It would be a shame to limit ourselves to that when so much more is within our reach.

Arnold Glasow, an oft-quoted American humorist, is reported to have said, "One of the true tests of leadership is the ability to recognize a problem before it becomes an emergency." The work of leading with a legacy in mind conforms to this statement. We must think about it now, before we reach the end of our work experiences, for now is the time to grow. Don't wait until it is too late. Engage your mind and move your feet!

Chapter 2

What Does It Mean to Be a Leader?

A leader is one who gives up all ideas of possessiveness, strives only for the well-being of society and holds himself forth as an ideal human being.

—SAI BABA

What does it mean to be a leader? This question has many answers. Perhaps the most common answer is the idea that a leader is a person who holds a position of responsibility—someone who is in a position to make decisions that affect others.

Another common response is the idea that a leader is a person who sets himself or herself up as an example for others to follow. This person may or may not have any formal power, and yet there are many who are interested in what this person is doing and how he or she is doing it.

There are many variations, but no matter how the question is answered, it is usually boiled down to one basic thought: a leader is someone who leads others.

I know this sounds like I am making a very obvious statement, but it is extremely important for us to examine this thought before we move on. This is because the very title of this book uses the word *leading* in a way that challenges the basic meaning that most of us generally accept. While I say that we accept it, I don't think that deep down we really do.

Consider this: most of today's organizations are designed in such a way that only a few people ascend into prominent leadership roles. It costs a lot less when a flat organizational structure is employed, and there is also ample research that suggests that self-led teams are more effective than those that are led through command-and-control strategies.

While many people want the opportunity to be a leader, only a few, according to the definition that we commonly accept, are ever in a position to be one, which leads us to consider an even more difficult question: Are leaders born, or are they made?

Your organization has struggled with this question in more ways than it is prepared to admit. I know this, because I have sat with the highest leadership councils in some of the largest global brands, and I have also spent a lot of time with some of the smallest family-owned businesses. Surprisingly, each of these companies, regardless of its size, is constantly focused on one common theme: How will we fill our leadership pipeline?

This question is frequently and purposefully debated out of necessity, because leaders retire or mess up all the time, and having the right people on the bench ready to step into those key roles when needed is essential for the health and wellness of any organization that wishes to be around for very long.

It is important to realize that most organizations are structured in such a way that only about 10 percent of their workforce is actually employed in what are deemed to be leadership roles. Now consider this: a recent study by the Center for Creative Leadership found that nearly 53 percent of the people in the organizations that it surveyed had been identified as high-potential talent and emerging leaders. Can you see the problem with the math? Nearly half of the people in the organization are identified as potential leaders, and they are certainly the ones who will eventually be promoted, but this means that only 1 out of 20 people from the complete talent pool will actually make it to a formal position of leadership within their own organization. This, of course, is assuming that no one from the outside is brought in to lead, which brings us to a very common realization: it really doesn't matter whether you were born or made to be a leader. Your real opportunities to formally lead others will simply depend upon whom you know and how much power those people have within their circle of influence. There are many who wait for that opportunity, only to discover that it never comes.

I know that a dose of reality can sometimes be difficult to ingest, but I want to make sure that we begin this process with one simple fact about creating a legacy: you can check your position and your title at the door. It is of very little value in this process. If you don't believe me, then please answer a very simple question: Who was the vice president of your country 100 years ago? I am quite certain that without the assistance of Google, you will be unable to answer. That's right, you are unable to identify the second most powerful leader in your country from just a hundred years ago. Don't feel too bad about this; Howard Stern and Jay Leno have humorously demonstrated many times over that less than half of the people they meet on the street are able to identify the current vice president by name.

Leadership's Real Meaning

In order for you to create your personal leadership legacy, you must learn to appreciate a more attainable definition of the concept of leadership, one that allows us to believe that all of us are born to be leaders.

I propose that the concept of leading is fundamentally connected to our personal and professional growth and development. We don't need to hold a formal role or responsibility to be a leader; this is because you and I are personally and individually responsible for leading with our own legacy in mind.

It is a good thing that what I am saying is true, but it is a bad thing that only a few people understand this concept. Imagine the impact on an organization's productivity and effectiveness if everyone saw him- or herself as a leader. What would happen to our measures of accountability? Would they diminish or increase?

For the purposes of this book, please accept the idea that the concepts of *leadership*, *leader*, and *leading* all refer to you and your fulfillment in the setting of your work-related experiences. You are the leader that matters. You are the one who is engaging each day and trading your valuable time for the opportunity to provide for your needs. You get to lead (work) where you want, so it is up to you to make sure that you are spending those hours in the most meaningful way.

Work is not always fun (that is why it is called work), but when we accept and honor our individual responsibility to be our own leader, then we can work in the spaces and places that are most connected to our individual purposes. With this mindset, there will always be plenty of work for us to do, because if we can't find someone to employ us, we can always create a business that allows us to work in this way. I repeat that the work that we do every day must provide us with an opportunity to do what we want to do. If it doesn't, there is no one to blame but ourselves.

What Is Calling Me?

Over the years, I have worked in many wonderful organizations. Once a very large financial institution hired me to create a development project for some of its emerging leaders. It was a very fortunate experience, because the company gave me the freedom to facilitate this initiative in any way that I deemed appropriate. Of course we had a budget, but my personal focus was on developing the firm's human capital without spending a lot of its financial capital. I wanted to make sure that we could deliver a highly engaged workforce with the least amount of monetary investment. We began with a small group of just 100 people. I knew that if I could accomplish my goal, then the work that we were doing would be made available to the rest of the firm's talent pool, which at the time numbered well over 100,000 employees.

I bargained for a very important principle. I wanted to make sure that the work we were about to do would be strictly developmental, meaning that it would be kept far outside the reaches of the firm's many performance management initiatives. My initial request was met with some resistance. The senior leadership team wanted to make sure that the areas of development selected by the participants would involve something that would directly benefit the organization. I successfully argued against this desire, and we were given permission to proceed with our plan with one simple requirement: to ensure accountability, each personal development plan must be shared with someone else in the organization, preferably the person who was directly responsible for each participant's work.

The project was off to a great start when we ran into a snag. One of the people involved had decided to use "weight loss" as the developmental objective. The person's excessive weight caused so much uncertainty that she felt that it was limiting her ability to be seen by others as an inspiring leader. I felt really good about the conversations that led to the establishment of this objective, but when the person's direct supervisor discovered it, and then shared it with the senior leadership team, the team members demanded that a more appropriate business goal be set. They simply felt that this objective was too personal and that success in this area would do little to advance the objectives of the organization. They said, "We are not a weight loss center, we are a business, and we are not paying our people to deal with their personal issues."

With the permission of the participant, I shared some of the intimate details of the conversations we had had while establishing this target. I wanted to be very clear about how her extra weight was affecting her ability to lead authentically. The worry about how others perceived her was a front-of-mind issue that never went away. I expressed a sincere appreciation for the goal and did everything I could to assure the firm that it would benefit from the actions that this emerging leader was about to take. My vociferous argument was eventually accepted on the grounds that this personal objective was very important to the participant and that ultimately the firm was hiring a person, complete with real emotions and feelings, not some robot that was charged with the duty of inspiring and leading others. I wanted to be sure that the senior leaders understood the value of self-leadership first. They saw the vision and the power of the goal; the work continued, and phenomenal results were realized.

Over the course of the eight-month project, this person lost 55 pounds. The rules of engagement required transparent conversations with supervisors, peers, and direct reports. They were engaged as account-ability partners, and the person was responsible for reporting her results and seeking feedback and feedforward on how to improve. I said that the results were phenomenal, but I hope you realize that I am not talk-ing about the weight loss that she achieved. This person became a true inspiration for many of the other employees. Her weight loss battle was well documented, but the most interesting result was the amazing increase in the level of trust in, and admiration for this employee. This particular person became famous in the organization for leading with authentic purpose. Though our focus never touched on any of the typical leadership strategies or behaviors, it did focus on the most fundamental of all: if you want others to learn and grow, demonstrate that you are willing to go first. The improvement in this person's ability to be a leader was dramatic—not because others saw it, but because this person engaged in a true act of personal best leadership. The company never opposed another objective. It trusted the work that we were doing and benefited from its results.

Too often, we worry about what we are expected to do so that others see us as a leader. I propose a more authentic idea. Instead of worrying about the many expectations of others, take some time to discover who your work experience is calling you to be. Wise leaders heed their calling and then act courageously, allowing it to guide all of their work-related activities.

Heeding the call does not mean that we will be promoted; it simply puts us in a position to make the most of the work we do each day. Remember, not everyone gets to lead, and not everyone needs to lead. Our leadership voice is expressed by our contributions to the work that is going on around us. When we walk with purpose, we naturally lead others. This is true whether or not we are burdened with a title. The opportunity to lead others must never replace our real purpose of leading ourselves first. This is the root of our leadership legacy.

Key Leadership Lessons

Through my work, I have discovered three common milestones that help us to make our work experiences more meaningful. The wisest of leaders pay close attention to these landmarks as they face the defining moments that so often accompany the fulfillment we gain from our careers. They live and lead with *service*, *purpose*, and *fit* in mind.

No one ever finds fulfillment in his or her work by asking, "What's in it for me?" By this, I simply mean that there are a lot of jobs that we would be unwilling to do, regardless of how much money we were paid. Our best work requires us to create something for someone else. It requires us to be committed to something bigger than ourselves. This commitment fills the wise leader with a willingness to serve others first; it ultimately leads to a better payday, but the payday is never the ultimate goal. It is simply the outcome that comes naturally from the focusing of our efforts on something that is larger in scope than our own individual needs. When we remember to serve, we find a greater connection to our purpose.

Many voices from the career coaching fields are constantly telling us to live and work with passion. Passion is a very natural result of doing something we love, but it can also lead us to the unintended consequence of engaging in meaningless uses of our time and talent. The personal best leader is focused on aligning work-related opportunities with purpose. It is purpose, not passion, that creates the fulfillment and joy that we seek from the exchanges we make each day in giving our working hours to a cause. Purpose motivates us to be disciplined and helps us to keep our work experiences centered on what matters most. When we align our work-related activities with purpose, we discover the spaces and places that fit us best.

There are companies that create some of the products that I love the most, but where I would never want to work. This does not mean that they are bad companies; if they were, I would not support them by purchasing what they sell. However, each company has its own culture. The founders created this culture, which by the way represents their purposes, around the products and services that they offer. The world is now free, and slavery is a thing of the past. Each of us has the opportunity to choose where we want to work each day. The wise leader chooses work in places that espouse beliefs and values similar to his or her own. The unwise leader thinks that this doesn't matter, or that he or she will somehow be able to change the established culture. When we find the right fit, our efforts to contribute flow naturally from us. This doesn't mean that things are easy; it simply means that the fit between what we do and who we are mitigates the challenges we must face in getting the work done.

The thriving leader is acutely aware of these three important milestones and pays special attention to them when facing the crossroads at each career opportunity. All of us can hear the voice that calls us to make our work meaningful. I am convinced that it speaks to us more often than we realize. We must never allow the volume of our business or our busyness to be so loud that it confuses us in our efforts.

There is no debate: we must work. But how we work and what we work at is entirely dependent upon our own choices and decisions. Our work sustains us and amplifies the fulfillment that we experience.

Mike's Leadership Story

I have never met anyone who models this truth better than Mike. Mike found himself enjoying a very successful career. He was providing for his family and creating a financial legacy. Life was good, and he appreciated his good fortune. His work provided him with many wonderful opportunities, but on the inside, he knew that it wasn't enough. He was searching for something more fulfilling. He wanted something more than just the financial rewards.

He had always admired his father, who had created a business of his own. One day he realized that his father was growing older and saw an opportunity to help him continue the brand. He knew that it wouldn't be easy, but there was a force that was calling him to leave his career behind and serve his aging father.

An agreement was made, and he jumped in without any reservations. He began his work by spending time with his father, which led to great conversations about the lessons his father had learned over a lifetime of serving the firm's clients. The more he became involved, the more he began to see why he was there. He knew that he was not just called to continue his father's work, but also called to make it better. Naturally it was a struggle to make it work, but eventually the struggle paid off.

Today, the business is thriving under Mike's leadership. His father is now 88 years old, and he still comes to work every day. Naturally, his father's responsibilities no longer include running the firm, but his voice still matters to the clients that the firm serves, and there is a role for him to play. He and Mike work together, guided by a shared purpose. They fit together in a way that is difficult to describe. The closest I can get is to say that there is a beauty felt in their presence that makes it seem as if they were always meant to be exactly where they are. This is true despite the fact that they both had worked in several different organizations.

You must be the director of your daily work experience. You may at times follow others to get things done, but you should never do so until you have followed your own voice concerning who you want to be. It is of utmost importance that you discover your leadership identity so that you can get the most out of your work opportunities. You will spend more hours of your life working than doing anything else. Don't be afraid to get what you want from those hours. If you are, you will always be looking at the greener grass on the other side of the fence. Don't be afraid of your own success. Jump into the job of being the leader you are meant to be. That is the beginning of leading with your legacy in mind. Ask yourself:

What is my work calling me to do?

How does doing that help me to establish my leadership identity?

The immortal words of George Bernard Shaw remind us that it is only when we jump in with true purpose, knowing who we are and what we are meant to do, that it is possible to find joy in our daily work experiences. May we never forget that, "This is the true joy in life, the being used for a purpose recognized by yourself as a mighty one; the being thoroughly worn out before you are thrown on the scrap heap; the being a force of Nature instead of a feverish selfish little clod of ailments and grievances complaining that the world will not devote itself to making you happy."

Chapter 3

Discovering Your
Leadership Identity

A leader's most compelling leadership tool is who he or she is: a person who understands what he or she values and wants, who is anchored by certain principles, and who faces the world with a consistent outlook.

—CHRIS LOWNEY

I met Eduardo in Mexico City. He was responsible for managing a $300 million sales channel for a well-known global brand. I was hired by his boss, the president of operations in Mexico, to strengthen and develop his own leadership capacity and that of his senior leadership team. Since Eduardo was one of his direct reports, it meant that we would be working together a lot over the course of the engagement.

Our friendship developed fast, and I was grateful for the trust that he extended me. It made it possible for us to experience some amazing moments of truth. It was a good thing that our relationship developed so quickly, because just three months after we began working together, Eduardo was promoted to be the president of operations in another country.

As he was preparing to leave for his new assignment, we met for the last time in Mexico City to discuss his aspirations for his new role. In our meeting, we considered some of the obstacles that might prevent him from having the leadership impact that he wanted to have upon his arrival at his new post. Because our trust was so deep, we were able to explore some of his biggest concerns without the fear of judgment.

This was a moment of great self-awareness, the kind of moment that each of us must face when we are truly interested in growing beyond our current limitations. As we spoke, Eduardo acknowledged a truth that only he could acknowledge. He realized that he had earned this promotion because of his success in managing a sales and distribution channel. To him, this meant that he had mastered many of the organization's management techniques, but had only a minor understanding of how to implement the organization's desired leadership behaviors. In a moment of truth, he said, "I know how to sell, but I do not know how to lead."

I was grateful for his having the courage to raise such an issue and assured him that this was a problem that many people face when they are suddenly thrust into a critical leadership role. Then I told him how uncommon it is for someone who is entering into a new role to be so aware of this reality and that his awareness would help us to create a plan to overcome his concerns. From that moment on, our work together was focused on discovering Eduardo's personal leadership voice.

Let me assure you that there is a leader inside each one of us, but those who hire us to succeed are often the primary cause of our silencing our personal leadership voice. The company you work for and/or its leaders are frequently promoting a leadership cloning plan instead of a leadership development plan. Your frustration with the lack of qualified behavioral-based leadership development opportunities is real, but you must not blame your firm for this deficit. It is very difficult and expensive for an organization to implement a personalized leadership development plan. In nearly every organization, there is a true desire to take care of its "most important asset," but many of the efforts that firms make often fall short of the ultimate goal of creating a vibrant leadership base.

There is something that you must realize from this moment on. It is not your organization's responsibility to train and develop you to be a leader. You are responsible for becoming the leader you are meant to be. Your organization can be very effective at teaching you what it wants you to do, but it will almost always be only modestly effective at teaching you who you must be as a leader. To be clear, what a leader *does* is within the realm of organizational training, but who you *become* as a leader is your personal responsibility. If you want to become an effective leader, you must learn to recognize your leadership voice. Then you must have the courage to listen to what it is telling you, then go and get the help you need so that you can strengthen the behaviors that you personally need to develop.

Eduardo and I spent the rest of that day and many subsequent days discovering his authentic leadership voice and his most effective leadership style. First, we searched through the lessons he had learned from those who had led him effectively and those who had led him ineffectively during his career. Then we talked about his vision for being a leader. I asked him to paint a picture of who he wanted to be. He was free to use any medium he desired. The only requirement was that he needed to express his leadership vision in a clear and precise way. I needed to understand what he was talking about. I knew that if I couldn't understand it, then neither would any of those whom he would lead in his new role.

I am amazed at how many new leaders fail to take the time they need to understand their leadership identity and to establish a vision for how they will behave, and ultimately lead, in their new leadership role. They spend lots of time developing their strategic operating plan, but they rarely, if ever, give sufficient thought to who they want to be as a leader. Instead of engaging in the work of discovering their own leadership voice, they willingly attempt to copy someone else's voice. It is extremely common for me to listen to a leader (and this is true both of those who are new to their leadership role and of those who are much more seasoned leaders) comparing his or her leadership style to either the good things or the bad things that a previous leader had done. As I listen to these stories, I can hear the leader justifying his or her own actions by comparing them with the successes and failures of someone else, so I am quick to remind him or her that in our work, we really don't care about the impact of the previous leaders. Our goal is to improve the leader's personal impact. This can be accomplished only by gaining a clear understanding of the person's leadership style and through the establishment of his or her own leadership identity. The lessons we have learned from others can inspire us, but we must be sure to connect with our own authentic leadership voice. This is the beginning of our leadership legacy. Your legacy will never reach its potential until you can clearly articulate who you want to be in your leadership role.

Who Do You Want to Be as a Leader?

The first step in expressing your leadership voice is the creation of a vision of who you want to be as a leader. This step requires you to examine your past and present leadership, but ultimately it will also require a thorough and careful examination of your future leadership aspirations. This is an extremely important step, because when you identify your aspirations, you set in motion a very important chain of events that significantly shapes your ability to create your leadership legacy.

In this context, your leadership aspirations represent the desires you have for your career. As you think about the impact you wish to make, your aspirations help you to identify the outcomes you want to achieve. No one else can tell you what you want; you must be the one to state your aspirations, and you must state them clearly. The question, "What do I want?" can be a real stumper. It takes time to dig deep within the layers of your experiences to identify your aspirations, but you must do it.

Because most of us are so busy with the business that we must conduct each day, many of us hope to find shortcuts by looking around, seeing what other leaders are doing, then attempting to copy their actions. This may seem like it is helping you for a while, but failing to identify your own personal leadership goals and aspirations will eventually leave you feeling empty. Consequently, your leadership style will not fit you, and others will see your efforts as phony. You cannot fake your desires—at least, not for very long.

Once you clarify who you want to be as a leader, it becomes natural for you to shift your attention to the priorities you will need to establish in order to inspire others to help you live out your vision. If you take the time to sit and consider your aspirations, you will discover that your priorities will almost always be easy to identify. They will flow freely because your desires will dictate them to you. All you have to do is give yourself the time that you need in order to discover what you really want to get done first. Don't be afraid to close the door and think about your vision and the priorities that you need to establish in order to bring it to life. There is another caution I wish to raise about your vision and your priorities. No matter how long you have been in your role, it is important that you revisit this exercise periodically. It must be repeated often because things will change and your vision will sharpen, and that will result in a shift in your priorities. Those who fail to reexamine their vision regularly often become stale and unable to inspire meaningful action in their own work experience and, even more emphatically, in the work experience of those whom they are called to lead. If you take the time to be clear about your vision and your priorities, your ability to lead yourself and others will thrive.

Your aspirations and your priorities form the foundation of your leadership legacy, and they represent who you are as a leader. This is the planning phase of your legacy, and the outcome of your efforts creates the baseline you need in order to define what success looks like and to identify what choices you will have to make and the actions you will have to take to ensure your continued growth and development as a personal best leader. As you work to increase the impact of your leadership footprint, it is important to realize that you must constantly be engaged in the process of understanding who you want to be as a leader. The desires you have for your leadership legacy will be more clearly in focus at different points during your career. They will grow with you as you mature, and as they grow, your priorities will grow, too. This means that the foundation of your legacy will always be a work in progress. It is not that it will change dramatically, but that as you grow, it will be strengthened in ways that you are unable to imagine when you are just starting out. Even the most senior of leaders can be surprised by how much their foundations are fortified when they spend time thinking about what they want and how they want to go about getting it. I repeat: this is a work in progress, and it never ends. A leader must always be growing, and it is the constant recalibration of our aspirations and priorities that give us the energy and the will to live into a meaningful career.

When we lead with a clear image of our desires and priorities in mind, we create the power that we need if we are to stay focused on what we have to do to become the leader we want to be. This focus shapes our choices and promotes an increase in our decision-making capabilities. It is extremely important that you understand the significance of this relationship. Too many leaders set out to lead without ever discovering who they want to be as a leader, so naturally the choices they make are disconnected from an authentic vision of who they want to be. Decision making is a daily practice, and each decision we make is made either in a controlled environment or in the natural chaos that emerges when we fail to lead our work-related responsibilities by and through a well-thought-out vision.

Some business decisions are made on purpose, and others are made in the heat of the moment without much thought at all. Each decision, whether hasty or well thought out, creates an outcome, providing fresh work experiences that, in turn, generate the opportunity for our direct reports, peers, and supervisors to evaluate our leadership footprint. The impact of this footprint is felt every day. If we are not careful, we may end up in a role or with a title that we did not want. Sadly, we may even fail to live up to our leadership potential.

In the same way that our leadership aspirations and priorities influence our daily decision-making efforts, what we choose to do will determine the actions that those with whom we share our work experiences will ultimately perform. Did you get that? Let me say it again: your choices as a personal best leader will determine the actions of those who work with you and around you. I hope you can appreciate the strength of the word that I am using to describe the relationship between the decisions you make and the actions of those who work with you. To *determine* means to decide on and even cause an outcome. When we make decisions, whether intentional or otherwise, we set in motion the actions of those who are within our circle of influence. I am always amazed at how quickly a work group moves to support even the most casual statements that a leader makes. They understand that their purpose is to support the leader's efforts, and most of the time they will follow without much resistance. If you say that you want to go to Chicago, they will get you to Chicago. The same applies to your leadership legacy, only the stakes are much higher. Whatever you choose to do or not do will influence the actions that the people around you will take each day, and those actions will lead to outcomes that will be either full or void of your own purpose and meaning.

You are responsible for making the decisions that are aligned with your leadership aspirations and priorities, and you must have the courage to stand up for your vision. Let me illustrate this point by simply saying that I have worked with many senior leaders who would have been more satisfied working in a small "l" leadership role, but because they listened to somebody else or believed the social hype about leading, they made choices and then took actions that resulted in their being thrust into a capital "L" Leadership responsibility. Normally, this resulted in a major disconnect between what the organization wants them to accomplish and their ability to find purpose in their work, which ultimately leads to the organization's calling someone like me to fix its broken leader.

When we begin our work, I find them in miserable circumstances, and they often blame those circumstances on the actions of their organization or of those they lead. It isn't until we start to examine how their choices and actions have contributed to their predicament that they can begin to see their way out. You are responsible for your choices. You are the one who is responsible for creating and living out the leadership legacy that you want, and please understand that there is no such thing as "no choice." Every action you take, whether passive, active, or stagnant, is preceded by a choice, and every action or inaction will contribute to your leadership legacy. You may not like the outcome, but your leadership impact is a result of the decisions you make. This is why I am urging you now to become conscious of the choices you make and the actions you are taking. It is easier to do this when you follow the leadership chain by allowing your aspirations to determine your priorities, your priorities to influence the decisions you make, and your choices to determine the actions you take. It is the only way for you to live out a leadership legacy that allows you to grow, to achieve, and to become the leader you are meant to be.

Our work must provide us with the freedom to become the person that we want to be. This doesn't necessarily mean that we will be able to do whatever we want. Work, by its very nature, will always surround us with certain limitations. As we come to understand our personal leadership identity, however, we become more capable of identifying the organizations, roles, and employment opportunities that match our interests and can provide the work experiences that we need if we are to grow and develop. Conversely, we are also better able to identify those that don't foster our growth. This knowledge then helps us to locate a workplace environment whose limits define clear boundaries that we can appreciate, instead of annoying and debilitating restrictions that constantly wear us down.

Eduardo's Leadership Story

After a brief interruption that gave Eduardo the time to establish himself in his new role and the opportunity to identify the key behaviors that required his critical attention, he hired me to work with him and his new team. His predecessor had been fired because the division's financial results were dismal. It was natural for Eduardo to rely upon the experiences that had allowed him to be so successful in his previous role. In fact, I am quite certain that his previous actions were precisely why he had been promoted to lead this floundering division. During our hiatus, he had focused solely on the numbers, which meant that he continued to behave as a manager instead of a leader. When I arrived on the scene, the members of his team were exhausted. They had enjoyed a few small successes, but doing so had worn many of them out. The minimal increase in sales had failed to inspire anyone. In fact, many were looking for a way out.

As we renewed our work together, we spent a significant amount of time holed up offsite in a series of intimate conversations that were intensely focused on discovering who Eduardo wanted to be as a leader. We focused on his personal and professional aspirations, which were largely influenced by the messages found in an inspirational book that he had long treasured. As we considered the personal impact that this book had made on his life and on his professional work experiences, he found the core of his leadership identity: he wanted his people to know that they were more important than the financial successes for which they were reaching. He wanted them to experience a work environment that was more inspirational than any other work environment they had ever experienced. He wanted them to learn more and grow more than they ever had before. From that moment on, we made sure that every plan was aligned with this vision.

We began a series of regular meetings with his team. The responsibility of setting, reaching, and following up on the progress of the annual financial goals was not diminished in any way, but the numbers became less central to our conversations. We even set specific times when it was forbidden to mention the numbers.

Under Eduardo's leadership, the team members carefully set key indicators to help them stay on target, and then they began to spend the majority of their time thinking about how they could make things better for the people who were giving so much of their time to ensure the brand's success.

One of the first actions that this team embraced was a simple exercise in recognizing the individual strengths and contributions of the frontline employee base. At first, these actions were met with suspicion, but trust was built quickly, and we began to see a noticeable improvement in the engagement of the workforce.

Eduardo presided over regular celebrations that were purposefully designed to recognize something besides the financial results. Great care was taken to ensure that these gatherings were authentic. The team became very creative in discovering meaningful ways to celebrate things that had previously been overlooked. These small celebrations breathed a spirit of unity into the relationships between the leadership team and the workforce.

I can't overstress the amount of time we spent thinking about how to keep these interactions simple and organic. We wanted to follow Eduardo's vision of valuing each person and lifting him or her up to a new level, but we didn't want our efforts to ever be seen as a program.

It wasn't easy, and our work required many hours of follow-up and constant vigilance in keeping the core of Eduardo's leadership identity in focus. However, these efforts were rewarded in a major way. Our collective efforts helped the team, in just a short three-year period, to triple its gross revenue and net profit margins, which eventually led to Eduardo's being promoted again to a new leadership role.

Key Leadership Lessons

Before he left for his new role, I asked Eduardo to describe the key learnings that he had gained from this work. He said: "Before I got in touch with my leadership identity, I wanted everyone on my team to be just like me. After I understood my core desire to help others feel valued for their contributions, I realized that I no longer wanted the members of my team to be like me. Instead, I wanted them to become their very best. My work became helping them to do that. Of course, we had the common goal of creating the financial success that we all wanted, but that was not our focus. Helping people to be their best helped me to be my best. I have never enjoyed work so much."

Please understand that I am not recommending that you adopt Eduardo's leadership identity. You must find your own. Because there is always so much noise around our work experiences, it may take you some time do so, but that should not discourage you from engaging in the process. It doesn't matter whether you are leading yourself or others. You will not get the most from your work experiences until you figure this out for yourself. As you work to discover your leadership identity and who you want to become as a result of your work experiences, please consider the following checklist and questions.

Leadership Questionnaire

Part 1: Checklist

List your three greatest strengths.

Now consider how often you use these strengths in your current role:

☐ Never

☐ Once in a While

☐ Often

☐ Always

List your three most important professional values.

Now consider how aligned your current job is with these values:

☐ Not Aligned

☐ Slightly Aligned

☐ Mostly Aligned

☐ Completely Aligned

List the three activities that bring the most meaning to your work experiences.

Now consider how often you engage in these activities:

- ☐ Never
- ☐ Once in a While
- ☐ Often
- ☐ Always

Part 2: Questions

Are you getting what you want from your work experience?

Does your identity at work resemble the work identity that you want?

How often do you take the time to think about what you want out of
  your work-related experiences?

Who do you want to become as a result of your work experiences?

Only you can establish your leadership identity. Dr. Lila Swell, an American professor at Queens College in New York, explained why it is so important for each of us to do this when she said: "Your identity and your success go hand in hand. Many people sacrifice their identities by not doing what they really want to do. And that's why they're not successful." Please take some time to think about this important foundation of your leadership legacy. Your success depends upon it.

Chapter 4

Leading Behaviors

Leadership behavior is not to be trained; it is the manifestation of your leadership wisdom.

—GRACE SABARUS

In the fall of 2009, I was engaged by one of the world's best-known banks to lead a series of personal best leadership workshops. The audience for this implementation consisted of some of the organization's senior-level leaders who were projected to rise to the executive ranks.

The timing of this engagement was rather interesting. We had just experienced the financial meltdown and the bailout of many of the world's largest full-service investment banks, and the U.S. banking industry was in the midst of a catastrophic collapse that would eventually erase billions in shareholder wealth.

The bank was doing the best it could to motivate its employees and develop its talent pool, but the difficult circumstances cast a feeling of gloom over our interactions.

On the day of our second meeting I received an early morning phone call from the sponsor of our work, informing me that our start time for the day would be delayed by an hour so that we could all attend a town hall meeting where the CEO would address the workforce. Because our meeting was to be held at headquarters, I was invited to attend the meeting in person.

At the appointed hour, the CEO stood and began his remarks. He was poised and full of confidence. As he carefully explained the fragile conditions of the world economy, he assured his employees that the bank had taken the appropriate measures to ensure profitability. At about the 15-minute mark of his address, he praised the workforce and actually said the words, "Our people are our most important asset." This portion of his address lasted approximately 2½ minutes, then he immediately launched into further conversation about the bank's financial results and reminded his global audience that the purpose of the bank was to make a profit. He explained that the condition of the economy had made it difficult for the bank to achieve this purpose. He spent some time discussing the impact of the losses the bank was experiencing, then said that in order to orchestrate a return to profitability, it would be necessary to reduce the workforce. Without a hint of emotion, he announced that before the end of the year, the bank would eliminate 50,000 jobs, and that a second reduction of an additional 50,000 jobs would occur before the end of the following year. Those in the room gasped as he continued his remarks. He spoke for another 15 minutes about the bright future the bank could expect and then left without taking any questions.

Shortly after his remarks, the meeting that I was there to facilitate was called to order, and I was presented to them with this simple statement, "And now Andrew will teach us about how to become a personal best leader."

As you might imagine, the attention of my audience was obsessively focused on other things. Some of the people in the meeting were actually wondering if they would make the cut. Their BlackBerrys were blowing up with messages from friends and direct reports who wanted to know what was going on and whether things were going to be OK. Their option alerts were constantly ringing as we literally watched the bank's stock trade from just over $35 per share to under $2 per share before the day was over. The crisis had hit these people in a very real and personal way. Their individual fortunes had been decimated.

I felt a need to be bold, especially because our topic for the day was the development of leadership behaviors. I pointed out that they had just witnessed an event that validated the importance of their taking responsibility for their own development. I made sure that they realized that their leader had spent 42½ minutes talking about how important it was for the bank to be profitable and 2½ minutes giving lip service to the idea that the employees were the organization's most important asset. I wanted to make sure that they could see what was being done to this most important asset: it was being cut in half for the sake of profitability. I didn't show them this to make them feel bad or to disparage the CEO. I just needed them to see the reality of the situation so that I could make a simple point: when people become personally accountable for the development of the behaviors they need in order to thrive in their work experience, they create value and become an essential part of the company. When cutting time comes, either they find themselves with continued employment or they have multiple employment offers from other firms that are quick to offer them a job.

Please recognize this simple truth: your organization will not force you to develop yourself. It is paying you to perform, and your performance is what it is going to manage. It has an interest in helping you become your best, but it is naturally, and rightfully, focused on making a profit. This means that most of its investment in you will be focused on the competencies you need if you are to be successful in your work assignments. Very little of its resources will be allocated to helping you develop the behaviors you will need if you are to be successful. You are expected to do that on your own. You will be employed as long as you bring value to the organization. If you are not known for bringing value, then you will be among the first to go when the reductions begin.

It is important to point out that this isn't just true at the office. Your family and friends will generally accept you the way you are, but they are secretly hoping that you will grow out of your most annoying behaviors. They will accept you the way you are until they get sick of the way you are, and then they will move on, too. They will never insist on your development. They simply hope and dream that you will wake up and figure it out for yourself.

The same is true in every other circle of influence in your life. The anonymous aspiration of "if it is to be, it's up to me" must become a motivating phrase in your life. You must be the master of your individual development. You must set the course. You are the only one who can decide each day whether or not you will add value. It really is up to you. If you aren't willing to do this, then you'd better update your résumé regularly.

Competency Versus Behavior

The words *competency* and *behavior* are often used interchangeably. This makes it difficult for us to understand how they are different, but you must understand the differences in order to successfully live up to your personal best leadership potential.

A competency represents your ability to do something successfully. Your knowledge, skills, and abilities were the factors that your organization considered during the hiring process to determine whether or not you were qualified for your job. Your competencies are the key indicators that are used to measure and manage your performance. The goal of all performance management programs is to ensure that you are carrying out your responsibilities efficiently. Your competencies are generally used to define what you do.

The word *behave* was originally used to communicate the idea of how a person manages and conducts him- or herself while performing a specific role. The word actually breaks down into two very familiar words, *be* and *have*. The prefix *be* indicates actions that are focused inward. The construct "to be" is used to demonstrate that you exist and that you are growing. In a sense, the expression of your innermost thoughts and feelings is the way you bring yourself to life. As you act upon these thoughts and feelings, you appear in the consciousness of others. Your behaviors are the range of actions and mannerisms that brings you to life. No one is omniscient, and that makes it very difficult for anyone to truly know you. Your behaviors represent what others can see. They are the observable actions that help those around you to know who you are.

Accordingly, there are two ways in which you can grow: you can improve either your competencies or your behaviors. However, only one of these growth strategies can help you live up to your endless potential. At some point, you will discover that your ability to improve your competencies is limited, while the possibilities of developing your behavior are endless.

Perhaps I can simplify this by saying that your competencies measure how much you have, and your behaviors represent how effective you are in using what you have.

Most of the time, what we do can be equaled or bested by someone else. This is why it is so important that we work on developing our behaviors. Our behaviors uniquely qualify us for our work experiences. They help us maximize our career contributions. Behavioral improvement is the foundation of your personal and professional development plan.

Most organizations publish a document that espouses the shared behaviors that they expect their employees to develop. This code of conduct is used to establish and create a culture that minimizes conflict and generates a happy and successful workplace environment. The amount of training and follow-up that is focused on these key behaviors determines how deeply they are accepted and acted upon by the workforce.

Sadly, most professionals labor for the majority of their careers without such a standard. Too many of them spend their time solely in pursuit of improving their ability to do their job. This leaves them rather vulnerable when any workplace disturbance causes their employer to reevaluate its talent pool. The only way you can remain relevant is to constantly be improving your behavior. Do you have a document that identifies the behaviors that you need to strengthen and develop so that you can continually bring value to your organization? If not, now would be a good time to create such a document. It is not as difficult as it might seem, but you may need some outside help to evaluate and assess your strengths and weaknesses. Once you do that, you will know where to begin and which behaviors require more urgent attention.

It is tempting for me to prescribe the behaviors that are most essential for you to develop, but I choose to resist that temptation because I understand how important it is for you to discover for yourself who you are and how you want to grow. As I mentioned earlier, each role has a set of required competencies that are the same for everyone, but the behaviors are what set a person apart in any role. Any prescription that I might make would be a biased prescription, colored by my own experiences and my own needs. You might set out to develop the behaviors that I identified with enthusiasm, only to discover later that they lack the power to motivate you because they do not fit your unique needs.

The real question is not, "What behaviors should I develop?" Instead, you must consider the question, "How can I figure out what behaviors I need to develop so that I can create the best work experience?" This will help prioritize what you need to do now.

Over the course of my career, I have administered the process that is commonly known as 360-degree feedback to more than 3,000 individuals. Through this work, I have helped these people discover the behaviors that they need to develop most. Sometimes we have even uncovered some fatal flaws and engaged in the corrective action needed to right their careers. Other times, I have used this process to help my client find a new place to work while gracefully exiting the organization with his or her integrity intact.

Key Leadership Lessons

There are some common characteristics about this process that I wish to share with you now.

First, I begin every feedback session by asking the person what he or she expects that the report will tell him or her. In asking this question, I have discovered that nearly 100 percent of the time, the person already knows what needs to be fixed. I am fascinated by the responses I get when I ask, "If you already knew about these weaknesses, why have you failed to do something about them?" The most common answer is, "I was hoping that nobody else had noticed." I can almost guarantee you that if you have noticed it, someone else has too.

Second, nearly everyone I work with, no matter how exceptional the feedback is, focuses all of his or her attention on the negative comments and ratings that are received. Rarely have I seen someone celebrate the positive comments and ratings. Most people typically cast this positive feedback aside without ever attempting to understand it. This creates a significant problem. Instead of building on their strengths, many people are instead focused on fixing their weaknesses. The fact of the matter is that you and I will always have weaknesses, no matter how hard we try to fix them. Our energy and our time are best spent in the pursuit of growing and developing our strengths. When we focus our efforts on stopping something, we are filled with negative energy. When we focus our efforts on doing more of what we do best, we are filled with positive energy. It is your choice. Which do you prefer? Which do you believe the people around you prefer?

Third, most people make the process more complicated than it needs to be. In any given feedback report, it is possible to identify several behaviors that need to be developed. No one actually has time to develop all of them, but almost everyone sets out to create improvement in every area of development. The development agenda must be kept very simple. I invite you to examine the behaviors that you want to develop and search for the relationships between these behaviors. If you search diligently, you will discover the one where focused improvement will have the biggest impact on your personal and professional work experiences.

Finally, it is common for many people to believe that they can separate themselves into two parts: a public self and a private self. I cannot express strongly enough just how false this belief is. Professional development is forever connected to personal development. Becoming a leader is not an adventure, but an inventure. An inventure calls us to explore the inner territory of our authentic self. This means that you must use your feedback as a guide for discovering what is most important to you. You will not lead with your legacy in mind until you learn to cast off the "should" that others prescribe for you and lead with your own voice. You are the one that must decide what matters most to you. Your leadership legacy will not be poured into you from the outside. Instead it must filter from the inside out. You are the creator of your own history. Developing your leadership behaviors is actually an exercise in developing your personal behaviors, which in turn leads to the development of your self.

Identifying Your Most Important Behaviors

I know the work of discovering your most important behaviors is difficult, but I want you to know that it will fill you with tremendous amounts of energy. It is a journey of great value, and it is worth every ounce of effort. I said earlier that I could not give you the answers, but I can give you some of the questions that will help you discover who you are and how you need to develop. The list of questions that follows is not meant to be an exhaustive list. Instead, each question is meant to provoke thought. It is my hope that as you consider each question, your pondering will evoke new questions that are more meaningful to you. Please consider these questions merely as guides that will help you to discover and develop the real you.

Who am I?

What do I stand for?

Am I ready to grow?

How do I want my work experiences to shape me?

What are my signature strengths?

In what way do I need to grow so that I can become my best?

What behaviors help me to be successful?

How can I strengthen my most successful behaviors?

Who can help me create and evaluate my development plan?

Creating Your Leadership List

I can't emphasize this enough. You are the one who must create the list of leader behaviors that you want to develop. These are your work experiences. The time you spend in your work-related activities is the greatest amount of time you will spend during your lifetime. You are responsible for the quality of your experience. Don't leave it to somebody else.

It doesn't matter how high or how low you are on the corporate ladder. You are still responsible for making the most out of your career. You must be your own chief learning officer. This means that no matter how close you are to the top of your organization or to the end of your career, you must still be anxiously engaged in creating and implementing your professional development plan.

A great example of a leader's willingness to constantly learn and grow is that of Michael Dell. You may recognize him as the founder and CEO of Dell Corporation. Michael is known for his hunger for improving himself as an individual and as a business leader. Given all of his successes, and they are many, it would be easy for him to say, "I am Michael Dell. I have created one of the most successful businesses in the history of the world. I really don't need to improve my behavior." But this is not his approach. Instead, he openly and sincerely discusses his personal development plan with the people who work with him to create the amazing successes enjoyed by his company. His leadership example makes it easy for others to follow. He inspires others to be personal best leaders and to leverage their behaviors, their talents, and their time to create more meaningful work experiences.

You may not ever get the chance to meet Michael Dell, but I can assure you that there are those around you who are creating their individual legacies with the same amount of passion and purpose. They must not be the only ones so engaged. Each of us owes it to him- or herself and to those we inspire to carry out this great work. Please take the time to discover the behaviors that will help you to authenticate your leadership identity. You will never regret it.

The development of your personal best leadership behaviors requires you to step out of the leadership cloning plans that organizations work so hard to provide for you. Though they are developed with the best intentions, only a few actually have a personal focus on your unique style and approach. David Letterman sounded quite astute when he captured what is required to succeed in this effort by saying, "There's only one requirement of any of us, and that is to be courageous. Because courage, as you might know, defines all other human behavior. And, I believe—because I've done a little of this myself—pretending to be courageous is just as good as the real thing." Legacy making is an exercise in courageous working and living. Behave!

Chapter 5

Legacy

If your actions create a legacy that inspires others to dream more, learn more, do more and become more, then, you are an excellent leader.

—DOLLY PARTON

What Is Your Legacy?

In Chapter 1, I used the equation Life + Leadership = Legacy to describe the relationship between a person's legacy and his or her life and leadership experiences. I wanted to make this connection so that you could begin to understand how your actions are influencing the ways in which others see you now and how they will see you when you are gone.

The challenge with using an equation such as this is that you and I gravitate toward quantities. They help us to comprehend value quickly. When we know how much we have of something, we are more capable of understanding its significance. Until we understand its significance and value, we are rarely motivated to set goals that call for action on our part. While it may be easier for you and me to comprehend the quantities we have, we must be careful to remember that our legacy is a quality and not a quantity.

It is important to remember that each of the terms in this equation is a theoretical construct. As such, these terms are nothing more than ideological concepts, which means that all evidence of their existence is subjective and not empirical. This means that you and I will experience them in very different ways. At some point, we must wrap our heads around the fact that while our legacy may be the desired outcome of our collective life and leadership experiences, it is not a quantity; thus, it cannot be counted by normal means. Instead, it must be felt.

For some people, the inability to count and measure their legacy easily prevents them from engaging in legacy-making activities. When they think about their legacy, they generally think only about what they will leave behind, and then they fall into the quantity trap, focusing the majority of their legacy-making efforts on the wealth that they may eventually pass on. While wealth is definitely one of the most tangible gifts that a person can pass on, I am certain that it is the least important thing that anyone will ever leave to those who follow.

Another challenge that often stymies the proper focus on legacy making (and this is a major stumbling block for many) is our common understanding of what the word means. Most of us readily agree that a legacy is a gift or an endowment that is inherited by one generation from another. I say that this perception is a stumbling block because it communicates the idea that someone else will enjoy the fruits of our legacy-making labors. You and I will not be here to benefit from their full impact.

Understanding this key component of legacy making generally requires us to plan for and think about the event that triggers the advent of our legacy: our own personal or professional demise. Very few of us get excited about doing this, so we constantly leave these important preparations for some other day. As we all know, the busyness that is incessantly generated by our life and work experiences keeps us focused on the things that matter least. Sadly, most of us either retire or die without ever having established a meaningful personal or professional legacy.

By now, I am sure you realize that the main purpose of this work is to inspire you to personally lead the process of creating your own professional legacy. Please consider this thought: your legacy is just as much for you as it is for anybody else. You must not see this exercise as something that will benefit only others. If you do that, you will fail to fully appreciate the original intent of the word, which etymologists agree originally denoted the authorized shaping and reshaping of a desired future outcome.

Legacy making is the ultimate meaning-making exercise. To fully engage in the process, you must accept the idea that what you do continuously influences who you want to become, which always yields a future outcome that will benefit you just as much as it will benefit anybody else. Your legacy is the compilation of everything you learn. It is something that you carry with you as you grow and learn to live up to your true potential.

Legacy making is a multidirectional exercise. As such, it encompasses your past, present, and future. It is not a short-term exercise. Therefore, as long as you exist, you will always be adding to it. Not only does your legacy represent your previous accomplishments, but it also communicates the impact of those accomplishments and portrays how each experience contributed to the process of your becoming who you are today. It is also a major force in shaping your future opportunities to grow and develop and serve others.

Discovering and defining your legacy requires you to move beyond the shortsighted definition that merely includes what you will leave behind. It is a forward-looking effort, not a backward-looking summary.

This may be rather obvious, but when we ponder what our legacy may be, we must be sure to examine what we have learned from our previous experiences. Unfortunately, most of us fail to do this. Instead of understanding how our key learnings have helped us to gain ground along the way, we are often found celebrating what we did or feeling guilty about what we didn't do. Legacy making that inspires us to get the most out of our experiences not only invites us to focus on what we have learned, but also encourages us to examine the present and the future so that we may discover who we are right now and who we want to become.

The question "Who do I want to become as a leader?" inspires forward progress and focuses our daily work experiences on the pursuit of deeper purpose and greater meaning. The resulting energy permits us to grow and develop in fresh and exciting ways, which brings us face to face with our true potential.

Leading with our legacy in mind calls us from success and into significance. It is not enough just to do something; we must create a force field of energy that will survive the end of our employment contract. The results of our work, the titles we hold, and the recognition we receive can never compare to what we learn and how we use what we learn to make things around us better.

Let's be clear about a very important point. Your legacy is about who you are, not about what you do. What you do will be remembered only for a brief moment, and then it will no longer matter because someone else will set new performance records that will surpass your accomplishments. Who you are and how you influence others will be remembered for a very long time.

Let's think about a couple of the most famous leaders of our time to help illustrate this point. You will recognize them as two great peers and competitors who were very similar at the starting line, but so far are proving to be finishing in very different ways.

Steve Jobs's Leadership Legacy

On October 5, 2011, Steve Jobs passed away. Just 21 days later, on October 24, his biography, written by Walter Isaacson, was released. The world's fascination with what Steve had done created an incredible amount of interest in discovering the details of his life. We wanted a personal glimpse of the man who had made our life so much better by creating so many wonderful things. As a result, Isaacson's book reached bestseller status in a matter of moments.

Steve made a connection between technology and humanity that continues to make it possible for many who are technologically challenged to profit from the amazing benefits that were previously available only to tech geniuses. He essentially erased our fear of technology and created some of the most amazing products. I write on a machine that was inspired by his brilliance. I connect with people through a device that he relentlessly perfected. He even changed the way I read books.

We thought that since Steve was such a master of thinking differently, we would discover that he was a relationship genius as well, but when the curtain went up and we got to examine the life of the man who had produced so many amazing products, we discovered a bully. As we read, we painfully became acquainted with a man who was frequently not admired by those he inspired. He regularly punished his coworkers with his abusive behavior, and his treatment of those he did not know was much worse. If you were weak, he could smell it, and he was quick to point it out in a most destructively public way. While he was doing this, he would try to convince everyone who witnessed his atrocious behavior that he was doing this for the good of the person he was berating. His life was messy and troubled, and he made his biographer promise not to hide that.

In one passage we read about a conversation that he had with one of his children. Here, we find him rationalizing that he did not have time to be a caring and present father because he was too busy creating successful products that would make the world a better place. Can you imagine what it must have felt like to be that child? Steve truly believed that what he was doing was the most important thing, and he didn't seem to care that this commitment made it impossible for him to become a better person. He thought the sacrifice was worth it.

He was distant with those he claimed to love the most, and only a few of those whom he led daily spoke of how he inspired them to greatness. Nearly everyone else stated that he had an uncanny ability to see a person's weaknesses and would use them to make that person feel small and irrelevant. The details of his abusive behavior toward himself and others minimized his creative genius.

Steve believed that the contributions he made to the world were his legacy, and so that is where he focused all of his time and energy. As I write this chapter, just two short years have gone by since he passed away. During that time period, new technological geniuses have emerged, releasing gadgets and gizmos that continue to erode the strength of Apple's dominance. Some people even believe that the company may have passed its peak and that it is now on a path that will eventually cause it to become irrelevant.

In the coming years, we may remember Steve Jobs the same way we remember the people who invented the TV, VCR, radio, cell phone, Walkman, and CD player. The amazing advances they brought to our world are now a common part of our daily experience. While we still benefit from their accomplishments, we no longer marvel at the impact that those advances have had on our life. They are now so common to us that we no longer remember the names of the people who brought these wonderful advances to life. Steve thought his creations could help him escape that fate, but his impact is fading quickly.

Bill Gates's Leadership Legacy

Now, let us compare and contrast the life of Steve Jobs with that of Bill Gates, another of the greatest technological pioneers of our time. On November 20, 1985, Windows 1.0 was introduced to the world. This operating system transformed the way we use computers and brought technological power to the homes of us regular folks. Since that time, many other Microsoft products and their updated versions have made our lives and our ability to communicate with others much easier. My writing is facilitated by one of those products. I think there are very few people on the planet who have not benefited from some product that was created or improved by Microsoft.

For 33 years, Bill Gates led the technological revolution. During that time, he worked many long hours and poured his heart and soul into creating what became an unstoppable profit-making machine. The innovations he led changed the world and even inspired Steve Jobs to think differently and achieve more. In November 2000, Bill resigned as the CEO of Microsoft, and the stories of his own leadership follies began to emerge. We learned that he was physically imposing and every bit as committed to perfection as Steve Jobs. Many people were happy to see him go because they felt bullied by his presence. His accomplishments could not hide the fact that his demanding personality minimized the contributions of those he led.

In 2008, Bill resigned from his daily responsibilities at Microsoft so that he could totally focus all of his passion, energy, and purpose on the Bill & Melinda Gates Foundation. This marked a significant change in his life. Instead of being focused on how his inventions could change the world, he began to focus on how his resources, and those of other highly successful people, could be used to make the world a better place.

Most of us are unfamiliar with the scope and work of this new organization. Yet, every day this foundation tackles some of the planet's most critical problems, including, but not limited to, helping some of the poorest global citizens to lift themselves out of hunger and poverty, advancing science and technology that is saving lives in developing countries, improving education and support to vulnerable children here in the United States, and building the alliances that will be necessary to continue this wonderful agenda in perpetuity. Now, Bill Gates will most likely be remembered as one of the most amazing philanthropists the world has ever known. He has made this his purpose. I am convinced that he will not fail.

Fifty years from now, the rising generation will not know or care about the technological contributions of either Jobs or Gates. It is quite possible that by that time, both of the companies that they founded will no longer be relevant and may not even exist. We can be quite certain that Gates will also be dead, but I am certain that many people will still be benefiting from his legacy.

You and I do not command similar resources, but that does not diminish our ability or our responsibility to establish a legacy that matters. The only thing that can stop us from making a contribution is our own selfish desires. We must never allow our weaknesses to define us. Our legacy is born from our strengths. It makes our weaknesses irrelevant. Our legacy cannot be measured by what we do; it can only be felt by those we serve.

Here are some key questions that are meant to inspire you as you engage in your personal legacy-making efforts. Please consider them carefully before you move on to the rest of this chapter.

Leadership Questionnaire

Will you be remembered for who you are, or for what you do?
Who will inherit your work and your legacy?

How can you make their starting point better than your own?

How will you carry your legacy with you as you move from one
   opportunity to another?

The Legacy Inventure

I must confess that there is a part of me that detests the idea that our legacy is only something that we will one day leave behind. I just can't stomach this thought. Our purposes must be much deeper than that. I am certain that my legacy-making efforts will personally strengthen me as well, and that I am the primary beneficiary. I work each day with this thought in mind. I feel it pulling the authentic me to new levels of growth and understanding. It helps me to continue to go on, even when I know that my influence in the business world is waning. I am drawn by the original intent of the word. It encourages me to see my legacy as a future-related activity that will breathe life into everything I do. This is certainly true when we think about our life after work, but it is also true when we think about life after life.

It is quite probable that you have never heard the name of Arthur "Deke" Winston. Winston started working for the Los Angeles Trolley Company in 1924 at the age of 17. He quietly continued his work at the company, which would eventually become the Los Angeles Metropolitan Transportation Authority, until he was 100 years old. During that time, he was never late, and he missed only one single day of work, so that he could attend the funeral of his wife of 63 years.

His work was to keep the trolley cars and transit buses clean. He worked for 41 cents an hour for the first 10 years, before receiving his first raise. He remained a kind and happy man despite being subject to the sting of racism, which denied him his dream of becoming a bus driver. He never amassed a fortune or created a product that changed the world, yet the bus yard where he worked was named in his honor. It is interesting to note that it is the only yard in the entire Los Angeles MTA that is known by anything other than a number. In 1996, he was even named "Employee of the Century" by President Bill Clinton.

What did he do to receive such an honor? Was it simply his work ethic and his dedication to his job that inspired these accolades? Was the naming of the bus yard and his special presidential accommodation the basis of his legacy? Hardly. Winston was a celebrity not because he worked hard, but because he influenced so many others by his positive attitude. It was not uncommon for men in their sixties and seventies to seek him out and tell him that they had been following his positive example since they were just little boys. He used his work experiences to make things around him better. He was never a capital "L" leader, but he led many people by his quiet example. One of his supervisors was reported to have said, "Once he arrives, we sort of know everything is going to be all right today."

It was his commitment to his values that inspired so many others around him. He experienced the ugliness of the world, and yet he constantly told the people in his circle of influence to avoid spending too much time dwelling on the past. He modeled his teachings by living them himself. His working knowledge of life inspired many others to see beyond their current circumstances and into something bigger than the difficult present moment they might have been facing. He used his grace and his wonderful attitude to live and love every moment of his life until his very last breath. He found meaning and purpose in his work, and he used that meaning to live a long and happy life.

He worked longer than most, spending his time doing what he loved. His work gave him the forum to be who he wanted to be. It is interesting to note that just 22 days after he drove himself home in his own car from his retirement celebration, he died in his sleep. Up until the day he died, he walked with purpose, and he was never burdened by his age. His straight back, firm grip, and sharp gaze inspired coworkers who were five and six decades younger. They wanted to be around him. They wanted to learn from his wealth of knowledge. Anybody could do the work that he did, but nobody could fill his unique role in making things around the workplace better.

You are working and laboring each day to make a few dollars, and that is an admirable pursuit. Your legacy, however, is not about what you are doing, or about how much money you are making. Instead, it is about who you are becoming and how you are influencing others to live up to their own legacy.

Who are you becoming as a result of your work experiences?
Is that who you want to be?
What do people think about you when you arrive at work?
Is that what you want them to think?
What will your legacy be?

Are you satisfied with your answers to these questions? If not, then it is time to do something about it. Please remember that you are responsible for becoming a personal best leader. You are the voice that will lead you out of dissatisfaction. The next section of this book is focused on helping you to develop the attributes and characteristics that will help you generate the most meaning from your daily work experiences. It is both a personal and a professional journey that leads to a legacy that you can carry with you as you move from following others to leading others and to serving others.

The following quote by Antoine de Saint-Exupéry may seem more about your life than it does about your career, but remember that you will work at something for your entire life. The only way you can fill those hours with purpose is to focus on the right things. This particular quote helps me keep that thought in mind. "How could there be any question of acquiring or possessing, when the one thing needful for a man is to become—to be at last, and to die in the fullness of his being."

You are in the process of creating your legacy. What do you want it to be?

The Arc of Leadership

Chapter 6

The Legacy Continuum

> Gardeners instinctively know that flowers and plants are a
> continuum and that the wheel of garden history will always
> be coming full circle.
>
> —Francis Cabot Lowfii

I am writing this chapter right now. You are reading this chapter right
now. I write with my present circumstances in mind, but by the time
you read this chapter, what is current for me will be the past for you.
Although this may seem like important information, it truly is irrelevant
because a legacy is timeless. It happens in the past, the present, and the
future. It is not a linear process. Instead, it is a series of circular adventures and inventures that are designed to encompass all of our experiences, ultimately defining our total person as it emerges into wholeness.
Your legacy is defined by continuous learning experiences that are shaped
by the recurring milestones of your life and leadership domains. The
present moment represents the opportunity for you to engage.

Today, as I write this chapter, my present moment is faced with another one of those very critical humanitarian and political nightmares that constantly threaten the peace and safety of our world. The brightest elected minds from all over the globe are at odds over how to resolve this crisis. A veteran political leader from my country, charged with ensuring a speedy resolution, is constantly in the headlines. One writer boldly stated that the way this leader handles this situation is likely to define his professional legacy.

This particular political leader recently celebrated 40 years as one of our elected officials. We know him very well, and much of his life history is now part of our public record. I decided to do a little research on his impact. I began by Googling his first and last names and joining them with the word *legacy*. It took my computer less than three-tenths of a second to come up with 6,500,000 matches. As I scrolled through the first 10 pages or so, I discovered more than 20 different headlines relating to various decisions that this politician had made over the previous four decades that were deemed to be legacy-defining decisions. All of these prior decisions are now long forgotten by those who are living through this present-day experience with me.

Had I kept looking, I am sure I would have found many more. Fortunately, a deeper search is not needed to make my point. Your legacy is constantly evolving. It is a movement, not a moment. Daily events contribute to it, but it cannot be cemented, finished, or destroyed by one single act. At times it will seem to be growing, and at other times it may seem to be diminishing; this is what makes it a living quality that can never be counted. It is not a finite quantity, but an unlimited and continuous reach for your individual potential.

I use the quote at the beginning of this chapter by the American businessman Francis Cabot Lowell to connect the thought of one's legacy to the growth of a flowering plant. At different seasons, the flowers appear and disappear, but those seasons do nothing to extinguish the life of the plant. It lives from season to season, regardless of whether or not it is blooming. So does a legacy.

The press of the current circumstances always appears to make other times and seasons seem to be less demanding or less important, but when we step back and put things in the proper order, we are able to see that the special urgency we feel is generally invented by our own egos. I am not sure why we do it, but we regularly fool ourselves into believing that the stress of our current moment is the greatest stress the world has ever known. Somehow we believe that our time is *the* time. To escape this myopic view, we must routinely hit the pause button so that we can see things as they really are.

You may have noticed that I have not identified by name the politician or the world event that is troubling me at this time. I do this on purpose because I believe that you are most likely facing a similar set of circumstances and events in your own time. The names, faces, and countries are definitely different, but the events that you are facing are just as threatening to the peace of your world as this one is to mine. This is how the world works. The crises we face and the peace we enjoy are constantly trading places and revolving in one great circle. Generally, we are concerned only with the arc of our own time, and that is what makes it so difficult for us to put things in perspective. Thankfully, we really don't need to see the full circle to learn from the whole. We can study our portion, and that will give us a glimpse of where we are headed.

Life is a circle. The experiences that you and I go through each day to meet the demands of our respective work responsibilities have been experienced by others who found themselves in similar situations long before we came on the scene. The main difference now is that the deadlines for producing value that we face have been compressed and accelerated. We must do things much faster than was ever possible before. In the past, people had time to ponder the purpose and meaning of their work and life experiences because they could easily disconnect from their work at the end of each day. We, on the other hand, are tethered to our work experiences by the leashes of smartphones, social media networks, tablets, computers, and the constant and never-ending updating of our favorite Internet pages. The strength of this virtual knot was meant to make us more productive, but we all now know that it merely connects and consumes us through its constant beeping and buzzing. We are never free from work- and social-related messages. Is it any wonder that we can't find the time to think about something as nonurgent as defining our own legacy?

Because of this press, it is difficult for us to see that we are actually part of the problem. When we stay up too late and work too hard to get ahead on the things on our to-do list, fatigue sets in, and then everything that we value gets squeezed and distorted, which greatly affects our ability to put things in their proper perspective and proportion. Naturally, the more overburdened we feel, the more impossible it is for us to slow down and find a quiet place to think about our legacy. Just the mere suggestion that you carve out some time from your already overscheduled day may increase the sense of stress and pressure that you already feel. All that seems to matter in the present moment is to get things done so that you can get some rest. It is a never-ending battle. There will never be enough time, or a right time, to work on these things until you make the decision to take the time to do it. You may doubt that taking the time to think about your purpose, meaning, and legacy will make a difference, but taking this time will actually renew your vision and energize your movements. Stopping to think about these things will always help you recharge your energy and recalibrate your actions.

The biggest obstacle is getting over the intangible nature of a legacy. Because it is a theoretical idea that is built by your own imagination, it can be very difficult to know where to begin. Even when we do, we are most likely confused by some of the questions that enter our mind. How do I measure this? Is it is even necessary or possible to measure it? If I don't measure it, how will I know if I am successful? Each question leads to another and another, making the whole process seem rather nebulous.

Legacy Arcs

Legacy making is a journey that is measured by what we learn and by who we become as a result of our learnings. We have already established that it cannot be measured by the quantities of stuff that we accumulate. It is defined by how we grow, and that can be especially difficult to recognize through our own eyes.

If we are not paying attention, the lessons that define our growth are often lost in the busyness of our days. Fortunately, there are some very familiar themes that are constantly emerging and converging, bubbling into our consciousness over and over again. If we miss one opportunity to learn, we can be confident that another one will arrive shortly. As we become familiar with the subject matter, we notice that the only thing that really changes is the degree of difficulty. It becomes clear that as we learn, our subsequent learning moments become increasingly challenging and advanced as we move from season to season. There are many overlaps between our personal and professional experiences, which makes it difficult for us to separate the lessons that belong to our life from those that belong to our career. But it can be done, and it is important that we figure out what we have learned or the learning will be lost.

It is also quite challenging, for reasons that were already described, to step back and see the whole picture. Thankfully, that isn't always necessary. Instead, we can learn from the parts of the whole that influence our individual set of circumstances. As we do so, we learn and grow and develop in surprising ways. Remember, because we know that the themes are regularly repeated, we get to look at the "parts" from many different perspectives as we spend our days engaging in personal and professional development. This provides us with the opportunities that we need if we are to deepen and increase the impact that we are making. When they are separated from the whole, the parts of a legacy are easier to comprehend. Growth is also more easily recognized, because when we separate the parts, we are able to comprehend a beginning and an end. This presents us with an opportunity to turn some of the characteristics of these qualities into quantitative measures.

A piece of a circle is called an arc. It represents a continuous portion of the circle's energy, and it is used to measure and predict the trajectory of the whole. The complete nature and continuous progression of a legacy is best comprehended when we separate some of the most influential arcs and look at them independently. The arcs that are separated and looked at in the following chapters represent some of the major growth curves that we must face over the course of our careers. It is important to recognize that they actually represent a continuum, not the simple plotting of moments in time. By this I mean that both the left-hand facets and the right-hand facets that I use to define the arcs are important. They help us to understand the sequence of the direction, intensity, and nature of our personal and professional growth, which is very often difficult for us and others to perceive. The totality of our experience—that is, what we learn from what happens to us as we move from one specified point on the continuum to another—is what makes it more possible for us to comprehend the nature and purpose of our legacy. This comprehension often contributes to the satisfaction that comes to those who feel complete and whole.

The chapters in this section define the leadership arcs that contribute the most to our legacy. Each arc is defined by two distinct facets, which assist us in separating the individual contributions made by each continuum to the whole of what ultimately makes up a legacy. True learning occurs as we set ourselves in motion, and in these examples, the facet on the left defines the early stages of our development, while the facet on the right defines the more mature stage of our development. As we separate these facets from the whole, we create the opportunity to examine the movement we are making as we reach for our legacy. There are many facets that make up the complete picture. By taking time to examine the parts, we improve our ability to see the whole.

It should be noted that the facets on the left represent our natural tendencies and styles. They also represent the behaviors that make us attractive to our employers, peers, and direct reports, but these behaviors do not shape our impact or create our legacy. Instead, it is the next-level behaviors that we develop as we pursue the right-hand facets that have the power to do that.

As we spend time learning about the personal and public journeys that are represented by each legacy arc, we begin to make sense of our work experiences. The first four arcs move us from passion to purpose, change to growth, goals to aspirations, and balance to focus. It is here that we learn how to leverage our leadership identity, ensuring its alignment with our deepest desires and priorities.

As we spend time understanding the shared nature of the legacy arcs that move us from accepting to understanding, discussion to dialogue, and listening to hearing, we learn how to better connect our hopes and strengths with those of the people we collaborate with in the workplace.

Finally, as we experience the transformative nature of the arcs that move us from success to significance, ambition to meaning, and growing older to growing whole, we begin to understand the true purpose of our work. This makes it possible for us to see the big picture so that we can use our enlightened understanding to better identify how our work-related actions are contributing to our leadership legacy. This helps us to know what to do so that we can effectively shape the future of our impact in the place where we spend the most time—at work.

Each arc helps us to understand the flow of our legacy. They are not the only arcs that are part of the circle, but they are the most relevant when we consider the contributions of our work experiences. It is not necessary to see these arcs as being closely connected in the greater circle. Sometimes the relationships are more noticeable than they are at other times. The most important truth is that each arc plays an important role in the creation of your work-related legacy. The more time you spend studying the obvious and less obvious relationships, the more positively you will understand your leadership legacy.

David Brower, a noted environmentalist and founder of the Sierra Club, used the workings of a river to help us understand how this flow influences our past, present, and future when he said, "We must begin thinking like a river if we are to leave a legacy of beauty and life for future generations."

What time is it? Right now. Where are we? Right here in the flow of the river of our legacy-making efforts. Enjoy your ride on the arcs of legacy.

Chapter 7

From Passion to Purpose

Passion is the mob of the man that commits a riot upon his reason.

—WILLIAM PENN

If you have ever asked anyone for career advice, you have probably heard someone say, "Just follow your passion." This idea may seem like good advice when we take into consideration the fact that the majority of our time will be spent in the workplace, but I have found that those who follow their passion either find themselves doing something that gets them in trouble or have a very difficult time providing for their financial needs.

Passion is a powerful word that is used to describe the way in which we respond to our strongest emotions. Ironically, the more we follow our passion, the more uncontrollable these emotions become. When you think about it, we really don't have to try very hard to feel our passions. We actually feel and follow them quite naturally. Sadly, if we follow them too freely, they become obsessions that can distract us and even derail our most important efforts. As Jack Kerouac observed when he penned *On the Road*, "My fault, my failure, is not in the passions I have, but in my lack of control of them."

I do not wish to suggest that being passionate is a bad thing. I simply wish to advocate the idea that those who think that the work experience is about following their passions may be very disappointed after they spend a few years on the job. After all, work is called work because it requires us to exert ourselves, either physically, emotionally, or mentally, in order to successfully perform a labor or duty. Generally speaking, all work is defined by a series of routines that we must perform in order to accomplish an agreed-upon result. As we engage in this process, we discover very quickly that these procedures were never meant to be fun or easy. While it is true that some types of work are more fulfilling than others, the more time we spend doing even the most gratifying work, the more our work can begin to wear us down. No matter what field we select, even when we select the one that we feel we are most passionate about, it doesn't take long for us to realize that because we *must* do it over and over again, it can become common and even mundane, and that this makes it difficult for us to continually experience the joy that we once felt before we decided to make it our occupation. I love my work, but it only rarely represents my passion. For this I am thankful, because I have discovered that in the times when my passion and my work overlap, and the weight of my responsibilities becomes too heavy for me to carry, I don't have anywhere that I can go to escape these pressures so that I can recharge my batteries and renew my energy.

Purpose, on the other hand, is a much more reliable guide. This is because it has the power to connect our actions to our values and to our reasons for working. Whereas passion captures only what we are feeling most strongly, purpose gives us the "why" for what we do each day. Naturally, this helps us to define the actions that need to be done right now. Purpose gives us the focus we need in order to ensure that the work we are doing is aligned with our priorities. Passion sometimes acts as a catalyst for creatively avoiding these important tasks. When we align our career path with our purpose, we experience more favorable results. When the bell rings each day, we know why we get out of bed.

Merging Cultures

I once was employed to facilitate the merger of cultures in a well-known global brand. The company that the organization had acquired had recently made an acquisition of its own. This meant that the firm was actually bringing together three very strong brands and well-defined corporate cultures. As the managers worked to create one culture for the three companies, they found it extremely difficult to get everyone on the same page. Too many people thought that they should continue to do things the way they had always done them. The problem with this strategy was that no one could agree on which culture should be sustained, and so everyone kept arguing for his or her own way, creating an unhealthy amount of chaos on the job. The difficulties were felt widely across the organization, but they were especially challenging in a new region that had been created out of several territories that had been independent prior to the merger.

There were nine countries that made up this new region, and the firms had previously operated autonomously in each. This allowed them to act freely in accordance with the distinct nature of each country's local customs and cultures. The organization had underestimated the significance of these differences, believing that since the countries were so close geographically, it would be able to capitalize on many expected synergies and efficiencies. The merger of the three very distinct organizational cultures, combined with the unification of these nine diverse country cultures, was proving to be a very complicated effort. After two years, this particular region was continuing to struggle, and the goal of finding a collaborative unity seemed far out of reach. Unfortunately, this challenge began to cost the organization some of its best people. Finally, a decision was made to seek outside help.

The purpose of my work was to recognize, develop, and bring together the individual strengths for the common goal of creating one united culture. I was very excited about this opportunity, and the fact that the people involved had been struggling for more than two years with very little noticeable improvement made the job even more compelling. The biggest challenge for me was that this region was made up of developing countries that were very far from my home, which meant that in order to get there, I would have to take some pretty long flights that left late at night and stopped many times along the way.

I understood the impact of this challenge, but I also knew that the only way that I would be able to accomplish the purposes of the project was to be there. I needed to be intimately involved with the people who were leading and managing the collective and separate operations. This meant that I had to travel extensively to and from the various countries, and for the better part of six months, I would be home with my family only on the weekends. The rest of my time would be spent in situ. This remarkable development initiative consumed much more than the time I normally allotted for work. To be so involved, I had to limit my other projects.

Before I accepted the job, I met with my family and frankly discussed the benefits and challenges that would come with the opportunity. I was very clear with them about the amount of time on the job it would take for me to be successful. They knew that it would be a difficult assignment for me and for our family. We worried about my ability to remain energetic as I made the weekly trips and the impact that this would have on our time together as a family. We discussed the pros and the cons, and then we established some basic guidelines that were designed to help us maintain the closeness that we normally enjoy. We knew that our time together would be significantly limited, so we focused on creating quality experiences that we could engage in when I was home. We even planned breaks in my work schedule so that we could be together without any other obligations. Stacy and I also planned a couple of times when she would travel with me so that we could experience the beauty of these distant cultures together.

I went to work, and for five months I traveled relentlessly. It was very difficult to be gone so much, and the hours I spent working while I was away required a herculean effort. Despite these challenges, and despite many other unexpected and unplanned family trials, we were all amazed at how much energy I had, and at how good I felt when I was home. My work was guided by a beautiful purpose. The developmental nature of the work sustained my efforts and allowed me to remain full of energy. My friends who knew my schedule wondered how I was doing it. Things just seemed to move along without burning me out.

Just as we were about to finish the project, a surprising organizational shift occurred. Because of the global economic issues that continued to challenge both consumers and manufacturers, the company decided to reduce the number of high-level leaders it employed, in an effort to cut back on its fixed costs. Unfortunately, the regional president who was championing our work was one of the casualties. The focus of our work and our results changed immediately when the new leader was installed.

His time was split between headquarters and the region, which required him to also travel extensively. Naturally, he had a different vision from that of the previous leader, and he really didn't understand the challenges that the region faced. This meant that he had a very hard time appreciating the work that we were doing. In fact, he had a general bias against all developmental initiatives, believing that they did very little to improve performance. It was clear that he really was concerned only about improving the numbers. He wanted to cut the funding for our project, but because I was under contract, he knew he couldn't do that. Instead, he decided to manipulate the scope and the purpose of our work.

As we began to move forward, he gave us clear directions to convert our efforts to a performance-based initiative. He wanted us to use the information we had gathered in confidence to evaluate the workforce and to help him with a restructuring project. Suddenly, the purposes of our work had changed dramatically. We were only six weeks away from finishing our original plan, and all of us who were involved began to feel a serious drain of energy. I am not sure whether anyone felt it more than I did. The long flights and endless nights in hotel rooms suddenly became unbearable. I was tired, and I found it difficult to focus during the long workdays. I just couldn't engage with the same level of intensity. I felt as if my integrity was being challenged with each request to deviate from the original scope. I just couldn't go back on the promises we had made. The trust we had gained was far too valuable to abandon.

As I thought about this, I realized that the only thing that had changed was the purpose of the project. I still found myself working with a team that I had learned to trust. I was still being compensated in the exact same way. I was still engaged in an effort to unify the culture, but the new performance-centered purpose of our work was one that I simply could not support. The job that had once brought so much energy was now physically, emotionally, and mentally draining.

I spent some time discussing this with the new leader. I told him of my challenges. I acknowledged his responsibility and his right to direct the work in any way that he deemed appropriate. Then I let him know that I was quite certain that if we had had the opportunity to negotiate with each other, neither one of us would have chosen to work together. Our focus, our means of getting things done, and our purposes were far too different to reconcile. It made collaboration very difficult. I suggested that we negotiate the termination of my contract so that we could both be free to operate according to the dictates of our purposes. He reluctantly agreed. He knew that there was a lot of trust between his team and me, and the circumstances were already challenging enough. He was afraid that my departure would result in the entire team going into a downward spiral, but he was unwilling to continue with the original scope. I promised him that I would help the team to make a smooth transition. As I walked out the door, I did everything I could to help the team support the new direction of the project. I couldn't believe the immediate impact on my energy levels. I was free.

A couple of months later, I received a phone call from this leader. He wanted to thank me for my willingness to support him, even when it meant that I would have to walk away from a guaranteed contract. He said that the team had made some progress, and that he was surprised by the many ways in which the work I had done continued to guide people's efforts. My legacy was felt, even though I was no longer there, and even though the purposes of our project had changed from its original intent.

Key Leadership Lessons

As I reflect on this experience, I recognize that I learned some very important lessons. When we are guided by our passion, we are almost always consumed by what we will get from our efforts. This is especially true in the work environment because our efforts are almost always financially rewarded. Our passions evoke selfish desires. There is no room for that in the workplace. Work is a shared experience. We cannot do it alone. We will always depend on others in order to be successful. Passion blinds us, preventing us from sharing and consuming us with the thoughts of what we might gain.

Purpose, on the other hand, reminds us of how we can connect our strengths to those of the people who work with us each day. It helps us to see how we can do what we do best in an environment that will most appreciate our skills and abilities. It focuses us on what we can give instead of on what we can get.

Much of the work experience remains the same, regardless of whether we are focused on passion or on purpose. The big and significant difference is the amount of energy we expend as we engage in our work each day. Purpose breathes life into our work. When we know why we are there, we want to be there. The money is never enough. We need to contribute. When we can't do that, then it is time to move on.

Our willingness to honor our desire to align our purpose with our work experiences is a major factor in our legacy-making efforts. It is the only way in which we can be valued and respected when we move on to other ventures. It is the only way for us to be appreciated by those with whom we spend the precious majority of our time each day.

The purpose of your work is not to be happy. It is to be useful, to be honorable, and to be of value to society and to the world around you. This is how we make a difference. This is how we become happy. This is how we create a legacy. We must never choose passion over purpose. It will only cause us to experience more struggles than we normally experience in our already challenging career paths. When we are clearly connected to our purpose, we stay committed and full of energy, even when the going gets rough.

Are you leading with your passion or your purpose?

What actions are you willing to take to align your work with your purpose?

As we journey on the arc from passion to purpose, we discover who we really are and why we do what we do. That is the foundation of our legacy. When we let purpose guide us, we are able to discern the growth that is needed if we are to accomplish our work.

Friedrich Nietzsche wrote, "He who has a why to live for can bear almost any how." Passion helps us feel what we experience in ways that make us feel wonderful, but purpose guides us effectively through each day. It is how we keep it going when the going gets tough, and it inspires us to say when we are finished, "I did that on purpose."

Chapter 8

From Change to Growth

Seek out that particular mental attribute which makes you feel most deeply and vitally alive, along with which comes the inner voice which says, "This is the real me," and when you have found that attitude, follow it.

—WILLIAM JAMES

One of the most powerful legacy-provoking questions I ask myself is, "Who do I want to become?" Whenever I am feeling lost, I consider this query, and I instantly find myself connecting with who I am and who I want to be.

Though this inquiry evokes powerful thoughts, merely thinking is not enough. If we truly want to become our best, we must be willing to move our feet. That means doing whatever it takes to get better, which generally involves changing our behavior and our way of being.

This poses a fairly significant problem. Let's face it: no one likes to change, especially successful people. Sure, we say that we like change, but for some reason, we resist it as much as we possibly can.

The only time we really like change is when we are acting as the change agents and inviting others to change. The changes that we prescribe always taste better than the changes that are prescribed to us.

Right now, you may be thinking that you know people who fit this description, but you really do like change, and you embrace it as often as it is presented to you. It is always easier to see the truth about things in the lives of others, but what I am saying is just as true for you as it is for me and everybody else.

You're not convinced? Please take a few moments, then, to consider the last time someone asked you to change or to do something that you didn't want to do. Did you do it? If you did, you probably complained about having to do it. What were your reasons for not wanting to do what you were asked to do?

Some of the most common reasons I have heard are: I didn't like what they were asking me to do. I didn't know how to do what they were asking me to do. I didn't trust the person who was asking me to make the change. I didn't have the time to do what they wanted me to do. I considered it, but it wasn't the best solution for me. If they had known me better, they would have never asked me to do this.

Whatever your reasons, and however valid they may have been, it should be pretty clear that your reasons and excuses were a direct manifestation of your resistance to the change you were being asked to make. Simply put, we don't like change. We like things to be consistent. We like to be valued for what we are already doing.

Reframing Change

Now comes the first dilemma that we must consider as we examine the work required to create the movement we desire on the arc from change to growth. Even though we don't like change, we understand how important it is. We know that in order to become our best, we need to change, but we still resist it. Submitting to a needed change is extremely difficult. We want to change, but because our pride and our ego are usually challenged by changes that we need to make, we often decide to simply stick to our way of doing things.

This is true because change is most often presented in terms of what we need to stop doing. Let me say this in a different way: the majority of the feedback we receive is focused on the things that others think we need to shrink or minimize in order to become more effective.

In order to stop doing something, we must first be willing to admit that what we are doing is wrong. Ultimately, this actually means that we must admit that we are wrong. Naturally, when we are faced with this challenge, especially in our areas of expertise, our most common response is to protect our image. Once our defenses are alerted, we dig in and inadvertently begin to resist the required or needed change.

Even the definition of change   to transform or convert—conveys a negative position. Very few of us want to be transformed or converted. We don't like it when someone tells us how we should be. We value choice, and we want to discover and choose our own pathway to becoming our best.

For whatever reasons, good or bad, change evokes these feelings. It is difficult for us to fight our nature and our learned resolve. Only a few of us can become self-actualized enough to embrace the changes that we need to make. This is why we need to reframe our dialogue about change. If we really want to become our best, we must learn to frame change in its most positive light.

Growth Versus Change

There is a better word that we can use to describe what we really want when we call for change. The word I am speaking of is *growth*. Growth is most simply defined as an increase by natural development. While many of us are resistant to the idea of change, only a few of us resist the idea of growth. We want to grow. Our growth is a symbol of our individual maturity.

We are much more open to growth, which is precisely why it is more likely to occur. We understand that growth, like change, is difficult to accomplish, but for some reason, we are more willing to pursue it. This is because growth is usually our own idea.

Growth is almost always framed in terms of what we need to *start* doing. Instead of being told what will happen to us if we don't *stop* doing something, we understand, without the prompting of others, how much more satisfaction we will have from our work, how much more productive we will be, and even how much more we will be appreciated when we grow.

We accept pain as a part of growth. In fact, we have developed affirmations to deal with the pain. Who among us has never heard the phrase "no pain, no gain"? We understand that we can't grow if we are protecting ourselves, so we let our defenses down and allow ourselves to receive the nourishment that we need, even when it is painful, so that we may become our best.

The pain associated with change is brutal. Pain is also a part of growth, but we feel it much differently, for as we learn and grow, there is also a sense of accomplishment. Sore muscles from growth actually challenge us to lean into the discomfort, because we know that we will feel better as we grow stronger. Change never breeds that certainty.

At first glance, growth looks a lot like change, but it is totally different. Change is externally motivated. Growth is internally motivated. Change is pressed upon us from the outside in. Growth emanates from the inside out. Change wants us to be like somebody else. Growth calls us to become our very best.

Accelerating Growth

Growth takes time. Before we can discuss how to accelerate it, we must consider the question, "How do we grow?" While the specific methods may be different for each of us, the answer is the same. All growth occurs as a result of personal experience.

Arnold Schwarzenegger is reported to have said, "No one ever got muscles by watching me exercise." If we want to grow, then we must quickly realize that the development of any competency or behavior is the result of the experiences we get when we exercise our skills and behavior. We cannot expect this development to happen any other way; there are no shortcuts.

The magnitude of our willingness to engage in our own development is the chief indicator of our growth. Our desire to be anxiously engaged propels us beyond thinking and dreaming, and deep into doing and being. There is no substitute for experience. It is the source of all knowledge. The way we feel in the midst of our work experiences provides us with the evidence we need to determine the worthiness of our growth objectives. If we feel disconnected and burned out, then we know that we are pursuing an inappropriate goal. If we feel energized and motivated, then we know that we are growing and working on purpose. It is just that simple.

To accelerate our growth, we must learn how to accelerate our individual and professional work experiences. Each day, we choose how we spend our time. We cannot expect to learn how to lead if we spend our time hiding in the corner. We cannot expect to become proficient at the skills we need if we are just getting by with the ones we have already developed. Our actions must be aligned with the competencies and behaviors that we want to develop. We must be focused on increasing our knowledge, skills, and abilities if we want to enjoy the work we do each day.

The mistake most of us make is believing that we cannot accelerate our growth. We believe that our experiences are time-bound and that we have only so much time. We fail to realize that time, by itself, means nothing. In other words, the only thing I can say for certain about this time next year is that I will be either dead or alive. The way I use the time in between now and then is entirely up to me. We choose how we spend our time, and we get what we put into it. Our commitments define our legacy, and our commitments are only as good as our resolve to learn and grow each day as quickly as we possibly can.

Consider two people who are learning to be more accountable. One person is committed to studying the principle of accountability for 30 minutes each day, and the other is committed to spending focused one-on-one time with supervisors and coworkers each day, discovering how to be more accountable and then applying what was learned to all work experiences. At the end of one week, there is a noticeable difference between these two people. One of them is remarkably more accountable than the other. The same week has passed for both, but the person who was reading about accountability for 30 minutes a day has learned and grown far less than the person who was actually learning from others and applying what he or she was learning in his or her daily work responsibilities.

The determining factor in growth is the rate at which we practice what it is that we want to improve. It is possible to produce results in a very short period of time, even if those results are normally seen over a long period of time. All we have to do is choose how we are going to spend our time. This is the secret of taking our legacy-making efforts to the next level. If you want to reduce the amount of time required to create your legacy, then you must be willing to accelerate the experiences that lead to your development. There is no need to wait for the years to pass; simply increase the frequency with which you engage in the behavior, and your rate of improvement will increase.

The behaviors associated with movement on the arc from change to growth can be grown only through your personal experiences. No one can force them upon you. If you want to grow, then you must be willing to work on growing all the time. If you are not willing to do this, then you will find yourself subject to the whims of change dictated by the world around you.

Key Leadership Lessons

In my work to help others accomplish the growth that they desire, I have noticed some very important guiding principles.

First, the growth you are looking for must be your own idea. If it is not your idea, you will abandon it as soon as the going gets tough. In that moment, you will say something like, "I didn't really want to do this anyway," or, "This was not my idea to begin with," and you will move on to something else. If you want to grow, then make sure that you are the one who is creating the plan.

Second, you must be willing to engage others and learn from their perspectives. There will be times when you will be blinded by your own shadow. You will frequently need the help of others to discover what your next move should be. There are people all around you at work who know. To them, it is quite obvious. Those who want to grow seek external feedback so that they can increase the speed and probability of their success.

Finally, you must be willing to apply what you learn. Despite what you have heard, knowledge is not power. Power comes to us when we develop intelligence, and intelligence is different from knowledge because it requires us to act. It is only when we apply what we have learned that we can successfully develop the intelligence we need if we are to grow and develop in the ways our work is calling us to improve.

The following questions will help you to move forward on the arc from change to growth.

Leadership Questionnaire

What is the impact that I wish to make?

In what way do I need to grow to make that impact?

What experiences do I need to have to help me accelerate my growth?

Who can help me by giving me the feedback I need to see beyond my
blind spots?

It is often difficult to identify the growth that we need to make. Because of this difficulty, we may decide to pursue growth for the sake of growth, and that is when we let the agendas of others guide our actions. This is a stumbling block that we must overcome if we want to live up to our legacy. We must be disciplined enough to decide how we want to grow, and then we must be willing to shape our work experiences in ways that will help us to accelerate the growth we are looking for.

There is a simple exercise that can help us discover how we want to grow. It might seem a little silly at first, but if you stick with it, it will connect you with what you really want and the purposes that will motivate you to do what you need to do.

Please complete the following sentence:

"When I get better at _____,

I will _____."

(Fill in the blanks by mentioning your growth area and one benefit that will result from your improvement in this area.)

Now, repeat this process at least 10 times, each time coming up with a distinct benefit that you will enjoy when you accomplish the growth you desire. Listen closely to what you want as you recite these potential benefits.

Do these benefits inspire you?

Do they fill you with a desire to engage in the activities that will bring about the growth you need to live up to your legacy?

Do you believe that growth in this area will help you establish your legacy?

As we move from change to growth on the legacy arc, we discover that we are the only ones who can decide what we want. It is true that we must consider all the points of feedback that are available to us, but eventually our actions must be connected to what we want our legacy to be. It is only then that we can sustain the actions required in order to grow. Growth is really a simple goal to achieve. All we have to do is experience it. You can figure this out for yourself and get moving, or you can wait until someone asks you to change and do things that you don't want to do. It's a choice that sounds like a no-brainer to me.

Chapter 9

From Goals to Aspirations

The measure of a society is not only what it does but the
quality of its aspirations.

—WADE DAVIS

et's face it: the business case for how an individual's legacy-making
efforts contribute to a company's financial results is still being written, and that is a significant factor in an organization's willingness to
invest in something that is normally deemed to be an exclusively personal
process. Consequently, many of the leaders I work with decide to engage
in these efforts through their own volition, and their resolve to do so is
driven by much more than the organization's hesitation. They understand
the personal and professional benefits of engaging in this process without
the knowledge or financial support of their employer. It gives them the
freedom to determine the scope of their work, thus allowing them the
opportunity to stay completely focused on their own agenda. Legacy
making is a personal development plan, and whether we are focused on

the life or the leadership part of the equation, we are going to have to dig deep into the realm of our personal development issues.

To fully understand the journey that occurs on the arc from goals to aspirations, we must be clear on the differences between the two. Your goals represent what you want to do, while your aspirations represent who you want to be.

Goals are generally connected to the boundaries or limits that we wish to overcome and the actions that we must take to overcome them. They help us to do more than we have ever done before. Goals, as we all know, must be clearly defined. Thus, we usually make every effort to ensure that the goals that we set are specific, measurable, attainable, relevant, and time-bound. We know that if they are, then we are more likely to attain them. Smart goals are the primary tool that we use to improve our performance.

Aspirations, on the other hand, are more intensely connected to our emotions. They represent the deepest yearnings of our hearts, our hopes for the future. They call us into action by breathing life into everything we wish to become. They inspire us to be who we are meant to be. As such, they are the motivating contributors to our legacy.

Our goals help us to narrow our focus and to close in on the outcomes that we desire. They help us make our desires more probable. Aspirations are open and expansive. They focus us on what may be, and they tune us in to our possibilities. It is important to understand this subtle difference: goals help us to close in on our desired objectives, while our aspirations help us to open up to possibilities so that we can live up to our potential.

Too often, we forget that the workplace is more than just the setting in which our results are created. It is also the laboratory in which we experience the most things that help us to become a total person. Work really is the incubator of potential, but for some reason, most of us find it difficult to journey along the arc from goals to aspirations, and this often leaves us feeling empty and incomplete, which makes it extremely difficult for us to create and live out our legacy.

Dana's Leadership Story

When I began working with Dana, he was struggling with this challenge. By all rights, he should have been more than satisfied with his work experiences. He was a partner in a highly respected law firm. His peers regarded him as one of the best in his field. He was highly compensated for his successes. His office was close to his home, which made it possible for him to participate freely in his home and family life. He had clearly defined the work goals that motivated him to improve his skills, utilize his talents, and increase his scope of responsibility, but something just wasn't adding up. Despite all the reasons why he should have been satisfied, he wasn't, and he wanted more. He wanted to live deeper into his potential so that he could expand his professional footprint.

Naturally, he felt that the answer to his problem was to set more goals. We spent a lot of time exploring that option before he could see that it really didn't matter what goals he set or met. He simply wasn't satisfied with what he was getting from all the effort that he was putting into his job. It wasn't helping him to live up to his aspirations. The good life was eluding him because he couldn't see the relationship between what he was doing and who he was becoming. In fact, what he was doing wasn't really getting him any closer to the person he knew he was meant to be, and that was the real problem. He had worked for so many years and sacrificed so much to get what he wanted, but he wasn't realizing his potential, and that made it very difficult for him to make the impact that he knew he could be making.

Once he understood this clearly, we created a parking lot where we could park all the actions that were focused on what he wanted to do. We put them there without worry, knowing that we could go back and focus on them again at any time. This didn't mean that he quit working on his goals; it simply meant that he was willing to allow the performance side of his work to run on autopilot while we figured out who he aspired to be. We actually started with the simple but difficult question, "Who do I want to be?" because he said, "I am still trying to figure out who I want to be when I grow up." Of course, for the most part he was kidding. But that expression of desire represented the real issue. He didn't really know what he wanted. Trust me, he is not alone in this lack of knowledge. Most of the people that I work with express the same concern, and they really don't know what to do about it.

Because we are compensated as businesspeople for the tangible outcomes that we produce, we are experts in figuring out how to produce those desired outcomes. Conversely, most of us have only juvenile skills at discovering what we really want. We like to save that for another day, and that day never comes. The problem is that our goals can create some satisfaction, but they have a hard time filling us up. Only our aspirations can inspire a healthy appetite for growth that fills us up by sustaining us in our actions instead of draining us through the endless effort to achieve the next goal.

Dana and I spent several days thinking about who he wanted to become as a result of his work experiences. We projected his retirement date and thought about what he wanted to have said of him at his retirement dinner. We thought about that date as the finish line, and we allowed ourselves the opportunity to dream about who he wanted to become without feeling awkward. I wanted him to get a very clear picture of who he wanted to be, so we were careful to eliminate any item that looked like a goal. We simply did our best to describe his future self, the person that he wanted to be when he grew up. It took a while for him to learn how to do this. We had to learn how to peel back the layers of protection that he had created to help him be like everyone else. Years of accepting and working on becoming the person that he thought his organization wanted him to become had left his true identity buried deep beneath the surface. Once he discovered who he authentically wanted to be, he felt as if a weight had been lifted off his back. He no longer had to carry around his false self. He was finally able to breathe new life into his work.

This meant that he was ready to grow. It also meant that he was free to let go of the work that was preventing him from creating his legacy. He realized very quickly that even though the firm he worked for was highly respected, it really didn't have a desire to grow in a way that would support him as he reached for the next level of his professional potential. The environment was conducive to supporting his reaching for the goals that he wanted to achieve, but it did very little to support him in his efforts to live up to his aspirations. The specialty he practiced was an odd and minor segment of his firm, and despite his enormous success, it represented only a minimal fraction of the total revenue generated. No matter how many accolades he received externally, he would never be recognized internally as a valued contributor. He realized that he had known this all along, but his fear of leaving such a respected firm had prevented him from acting on what he knew he must do. This realization freed him to entertain offers from other firms that were globally recognized in his field and whose purposes were aligned with his own aspirations.

Dana wanted the opportunity to live up to his potential, and that desire eventually led him to leave his firm and accept a leadership responsibility at a firm that would stretch him and allow him to become who he wanted to be.

This required him to make many sacrifices. His new office was located on the other side of the city, which meant that he had to endure a long commute each morning and night. His new role provided him with an opportunity to lead others, and that meant that he was able to leverage his experiences to guide them through their own challenges. The headquarters of his new firm were located in a faraway city, and that meant that his travel schedule increased. His revenue target was more aggressive than his previous revenue goal had been, and that meant that he would have to work more hours, at least in the beginning, to accomplish the goals his company had set for him. All of these things and many others took more time out of his day, but they also provided him with the opportunity to become the person he wanted to be.

Naturally, we spent quite a bit of time evaluating this new idea before he accepted the offer. There were days when it was a definite no, and others when it was a hardy yes. He quietly got feedback from many people that he trusted, and their levels of support for the decision were mixed. Some thought he would be crazy to leave, and others thought he would be crazy to stay.

The fact that we had begun by identifying his aspirations made it possible for us to use those aspirations as a guide for the action he would ultimately take. We knew who he wanted to be, so we could pick the actions and the employment that would provide the greatest opportunities for him to become that person.

Because we had taken the time to do this work before a decision needed to be made, he had the right information when it was time for him to make the decision, and this eventually allowed him to make the right decision. We knew this for sure when, after a couple of years had passed, he was still satisfied with the decision he had made. Following his aspirations had brought him more meaning than he had ever experienced in the many goal attainments he had enjoyed. He finally felt that he was living up to his professional potential.

Key Leadership Lessons

When I speak to people about Dana's decision, they almost always think that it indicates that if they want to live up to their own potential, they will probably need to leave their current employment. This is not the lesson I wish you to learn. One of the things I have discovered is that most people have done very little to become acquainted with their personal and professional aspirations. The truth is that you will never understand the actions that you may need to take until you identify the aspirations that will sustain those actions after you make them. Your personal and professional desires must always be the source of your aspirations. The transition from goals to aspirations begins with the exercise of identifying how you will breathe life into your work. You must be clear on this before you can make any decisions.

Once you have done that, you can begin to evaluate your job and the work you do each day. More often than not, the people I work with discover that their organization is already offering pathways that are perfectly aligned with their own aspirations. They didn't know that these pathways existed before because they had not taken the time to understand their own aspirations clearly. Once they did that, they were prepared to receive the support that was always available to them. I am never surprised to see how quickly their sense of belonging improves or how much more value they bring to their firm. When you evaluate your current role, you must be willing to see it with fresh eyes. That means that you may have to realize the ways in which you have been sabotaging your own potential. Your aspirations will help you do that.

The arc from goals to aspirations calls us to answer the question of who we want to be. It can be a scary question because it may require you to let go of the possessions, and maybe even the profession, that you have used for so long to define yourself. It is important that you allow yourself the opportunity to conduct this search. It is one of the most essential paths leading to your legacy.

Ask yourself a few simple questions to help you get started, and then allow yourself the freedom to explore the new questions that will emerge as you think about your professional aspirations. This takes time. Don't deny yourself the luxury or the pleasure of considering these questions. You will know when you are on the right track when you begin to feel a new energy in your work. This energy is similar to the energy you felt when you first decided on your career, but it is different in the sense that it will help you see how you can use your career and your work experiences to become the total person that you long to be. Your aspirations help you feel whole.

Leadership Questionnaire

Who do you want to be?

Who is your work calling you to become?

Without worrying about who is watching, what are the genuine aspirations that represent your reach toward your professional potential?

What must you do to step out of the alternative you that you have allowed to exist in the name of goal attainment? How can you use the lessons you learned from those experiences to help you define the authentic you that you aspire to become?

It is easy to worry about what others will think when you begin the journey on the arc from goals to aspirations. As I mentioned, some of Dana's friends told him that they thought he was crazy when he announced his plans to start a new adventure. They worried that he was having some sort of a midlife crisis. However, what we both found to be most interesting was the way in which they would critique his decision in one breath, but in the very next breath declare that they wished they had the courage to do what he was doing. We knew then that he was moving his career in the right direction.

Your opportunity to craft your legacy is highly influenced by your willingness to stare deeply into your aspirations and then follow those dreams. Don't wait to examine them. Just take a few moments now to see who it is that you want to become, and then use that vision to plan your next steps. You will never work long enough to regret that decision.

When we allow our aspirations to guide us, we begin to connect to what really gives us life. It is not what we do that gives us life; it is the pursuit of becoming the person we are meant to be. There is a noticeable difference when you work with people who have already figured this out. They are creating a legacy that inspires others to follow their own professional aspirations, too. Be such a person at your work. Give the people around you permission to live up to their own aspirations by showing them your willingness to live up to your own. This is how you will get the most from your work experiences. Just do it!

Chapter 10

From Balance to Focus

"Here's a nice image for a life in balance," she said. "You're juggling these four balls that you've named work, family, friends, spirit. Now, work is a rubber ball. If you drop it, it bounces back. The other balls they're made of glass. I've dropped a few of those glass balls in my day. Sometimes they chip, sometimes they shatter to pieces."

—James Patterson

247,000,000. That was how many hits I got today when I Googled the phrase "work/life balance." Obviously this topic is extremely relevant to our legacy-making efforts. Everyone is wondering how he or she can balance the trade-offs between the personal and professional realms that have to be made each day.

As a father of seven children, I can say that I am something of an expert on this topic. Not the kind of expert that necessarily knows all the answers, but I certainly know the questions, and my work and life experiences have taught me many of the answers, too.

The arc from balance to focus is definitely one of the most interesting and intriguing journeys on the pathway to our legacy. When we feel dissatisfied with the quality of our life, then we also feel tired and disengaged at work. We think that the solution to this problem is to spend more time at home, but those of us who have tried this have found little relief. There are many people who champion the quest for balance, but very few who report having a sense of balance in their life. Despite the fact that organizations continue to do everything they can to create flexible working arrangements, most employees simply find the consequences of working flexibly to be too great. The time away does little to relieve the pressure they feel when they come back to the office. When they return, they are behind in their responsibilities, and they feel obligated to work longer hours so that they can catch up. But let's be honest: who ever really gets away anymore, anyway? Most clients I work with generally have no fewer than 300 e-mails in their inbox waiting for their response.

A research study focused on the work/life balance habits of the U.S. workforce, published in 2013 by Korn/Ferry International, reported that an astounding 94 percent of those surveyed believed that working from home is an important option, especially for parents who work. However, despite this overwhelming response rate, the survey also found that while the respondents understood the benefits of working from home for both companies and workers, they felt that doing this limited their career advancement opportunities. In other words, the benefits were there, but they came at a price that was too steep for most people to accept. They knew that if they worked from home, they would become invisible to the organization.

Another study found that 89 percent of Americans think that work/life balance is a problem, with 54 percent calling it a "significant" problem. This issue will always be on the front burner, but as long as we seek balance, we will be disappointed.

My Story

In 2004, my home and work experiences taught me an important lesson about the search for work/life balance. During that year, I was nurturing a two-year-old company that was experiencing critical growth. In addition, I was enrolled in 52 credit hours of graduate school courses in the pursuit of completing my PhD. On the home front, we were in the middle of a significant remodeling of our home, and my wife was pregnant with our sixth child.

We seemed to be handling things pretty efficiently, and then crisis struck. Stacy, my wife, was diagnosed with a condition that threatened both her health and the health of our baby. She was advised to stay in bed for the remainder of the pregnancy. This diagnosis came to us in the first trimester, so in a sense, it was a sentence of seven months in bed at one of the busiest times of our lives.

In a single moment, I became responsible for everything that was on our busy calendar. I had to be both the mom and the dad for our children, the student and the professional at work, and the general contractor on the remodeling at home. It was the most demanding time of my life. The days were never long enough to get everything done; the idea of work/life balance was nothing more than a vacant wish. There really was no margin for error. I had to use every hour efficiently, or else suffer the consequences.

During this time period, I discovered a truth that many people find difficult to accept: work/life balance is a myth. There really is no such thing. I am sure there will be many who will argue with this premise, but I would ask them to explain why it is that in a time when we continue to invest more research and training in this area, nearly every study finds the respondents continually reporting their inability to gain a sense of balance in their lives. Obviously, we are focusing on the wrong things.

Discovering this fact should not disempower us. Actually, it is the opposite that occurs. This is because balance actually comes naturally to us. We are never really out of balance. This is because our body, mind, and spirit are perfect regulators of our actions. When we feel out of balance, we shut down or divert our focus to something else. It is only when we make balance the primary indicator of our happiness that we begin to feel a decrease in our well-being. I repeat, balance is the natural result of every movement we make. When we set things in motion, we discover how to balance.

Think of your experience with something as simple, at least for most of us, as walking. Do you really have to think about balancing yourself when you stand up, walk, or run? My experience is that unless there is something physically wrong with us, very few of us actually pause to think about what it takes to balance our bodies when we are engaged in this activity. We know what to do instinctively. We simply walk without thinking, and that is actually our problem. In order to be effective, we must think about our movement—not from the perspective of balance, but from the perspective of direction. It is not our balance that we must check, but our focus on where we are going. If we are heading in the right direction, then we feel satisfied. If we are moving counter to our purposes and values, then it really won't matter how balanced we actually are; we will still feel dissatisfied.

Our efforts must be focused on the things that really matter. It is the only way we will feel the benefit of our natural equilibrium. Anything else will leave us feeling unsettled.

Working with Marshall

This is true no matter how successful we may become. During the personal crisis just described, I was privileged to have Marshall Goldsmith as one of my clients. At the time, Marshall was ranked by *Forbes* magazine as the number one executive coach in the world, and since that time, he has also been ranked by Thinkers50 as the as one of the most influential business thinkers of our time. His successes are astounding. He is free to select the work experiences that he wants, and his family is very important to him. Despite all of his successes and intentions, however, he recognized that he needed help in maintaining a proper focus. His business and his busyness made it easy for him to be distracted and to focus on the things that mattered least. I hope you will appreciate that I am saying "the things that mattered least." This is done on purpose to communicate the fact that most of what occupies our focus are the things that matter least. They are often the most pressing things. They make us feel as if we are constantly in the middle of an emergency. They take us away from what really matters. They make it hard for us to get back to what really matters. These things matter, but they are the things that matter least, and we let them get in the way because it feels like there will be huge short-term worries if we don't.

Obviously, Marshall was already a very successful individual. He did not need my help in figuring out what he needed to do. Instead, he needed help in figuring out how to consistently do what he already knew he needed to do. He actually wanted to do more, but he knew that he couldn't do that until he figured out how to align his actions with the things he wanted and needed to focus on doing.

We began our work with a very simple strategy. My job was to call Marshall every day at 10:00 p.m., no matter where he was in the world, and ask him a series of focusing questions. His job was to create the questions that I would ask him during our call. He was responsible for developing questions that would inspire him to take action. Each question was carefully evaluated and rated for its potential to focus Marshall on those things that produced very little short-term benefit, but that when done over time would produce extremely significant long-term benefits.

If the question added little or no value to this objective, we didn't spend time asking it.

Immediately, Marshall began to feel the impact of these questions. The chaos of a life spent traveling the world to help successful people become even more successful began to find order. Not only did Marshall report a greater sense of well-being, but he also reported greater levels of productivity. We never once spent so much as a minute of our time talking about balance, even when he felt unbalanced. Instead, we directed our efforts toward the things that he really needed to focus on each day. We made sure that those things got done first. It didn't matter where he was or how much time he spent doing these things. We just wanted to make sure that he was paying daily attention to the things that really mattered to him, and that is what made the difference. I don't think he ever reported that he was feeling more balance; in the end, that really didn't matter.

Here is how he describes the experience in his own words:

Why does this process work so well? For one, it forces me to confront how I actually live my values every single day. I either believe that something matters or I don't. If I believe it, I can put it on the list and do it! If I really don't want to do it, I can face reality, quit kidding myself, and take it off my list.

Marshall and I average about three minutes a day going over his most important questions. Some of our calls actually last just a little over 90 seconds. The results of this process are not determined by the amount of time we spend together. Instead, they are determined by the frequency of asking the questions that focus him on his real goals and aspirations. Marshall knows that I am going to call him every day, so he works hard on what really matters so that he will be able to report positive results. Knowing that I am going to call him, and that he is going to report on his day and be accountable for his actions, serves as a strong motivation to stay focused each day on what really matters.

Over the past 25 years, I have employed this simple process with many of my clients. It is a profound process because it helps us move along the arc from balance to focus.

Key Leadership Lessons

My work with Marshall that began during one of the most chaotic periods of my life helped me to realize some very simple and vital lessons

First, balance is not the goal. This is not simply because it is impossible, but more because of the reality that there will always be urgencies and emergencies in our lives that will make us feel as if we are out of balance. Fortunately, we find our balance quickly and naturally. All we have to do is move our feet.

Focus is the goal. Each day, we must take the time to think about the things that matter most and then purposefully plan the activities that will help us accomplish those things. If we do this, we will be in balance, even when we are faced with competing interests. Our planning will help us maintain alignment in everything that we do.

Finally, I discovered that it is important to have an accountability partner. This person will help us stay on track when we get lost. Marshall understands the concept of staying focused better than anyone I have ever met, yet he still employs me to help him stay focused. All of us need help, and it is easy to find.

Please consider the following questions and the reflection exercise as a way to help you find the focus you need, then enroll somebody to help you maintain it. You can get from this chapter only what you take out of it. Now is the time to capture your thoughts and discoveries. Do it before they fade away!

Leadership Questionnaire

Am I willing to let go of the myth of balance so that I can work on
  bringing into focus what really matters in my life?

What are the key areas that require my focus?

How will I make sure that I spend time each day focusing on these
  areas?

What strengths can I use to support my growth?

Whom can I enroll to help me?

Exercise

Imagine that a friend of yours is going to call you every night and ask
you questions about your work and your life. What questions would you
want this person to ask?

Write down the questions that you want your friend to ask you. Even
engaging in this simple part of the process will help you better understand
your own values and how you can improve your focus.

Now be courageous. Recruit a friend to start asking you these questions every day. Keep track of your results and review them often. Be
as serious about this as you are about the other key indicators you are
tracking at work.

There is a warning that I must issue on this particular legacy arc.
While the warning definitely applies to all the other legacy arcs as well,
I find it to be most important in this particular case.

Too many people find it easy to argue that the differences between
balance and focus are imperceptible. They argue that these differences
cannot really add to our legacy-making efforts. If this is your argument,
then let me remind you that balance is the act of putting something into
a steady position so that it does not fall. It is impossible for anyone to put
his or her work and life experiences into that position. Each and every

day we will fall short of our ideals. Finding more balance may be impossible, but we can all find the time to fine-tune our focus. Focus gives us a sharpness of vision, which increases our understanding. We need that increase so that we can create a legacy that will endure the chaos of our busy life. Once again, this is a conversation that is focused on quality rather than quantity and that offers us the opportunity to grow. Growth is not a given; it is earned by those who relentlessly sharpen their focus on the things that really matter. Do you have your legacy in sight? Now is the time to bring it into focus.

I love this quote from Reggie Leach, a former NHL player from Canada. He is fond of reminding us, "Success is not the result of spontaneous combustion. We must set ourself on fire." It is your responsibility to move freely on this legacy arc. Only you can determine what your focus must be. Light the match.

Chapter 11

From Accepting to Understanding

Accepting all the good and bad about someone. It's a great
thing to aspire to. The hard part is actually doing it.

—SARAH DESSEN

The past 25 years have presented me with regular opportunities to engage in many diversity initiatives, most of which have failed miserably. I hesitate to say that they failed, because I know what this admission implies. Too many people receive the news of these failures and interpret them to mean that the purposes of diversity are flawed. They use this interpretation to interrupt, disrupt, and even terminate current and future projects. We need to promote diversity. When we do, we have a better workforce.

The challenge is in figuring out what diversity means, where it appears, how it is best recognized, and how we can use it in the most effective way. These questions have been asked for a while, but my experience is that the agenda almost always ends up focusing on how we can fill more positions with people of a certain race, gender, or sexual orientation. This is a confusing agenda, and it invites strife in almost every situation where it is employed. To many people, it seems as if what is actually being said is that unless you are one of the designated type, you must change places and take a seat on the outside looking in. For some people, it seems like it is about time that we begin to do something about all the injustices that continue to exist in the workplace.

Perhaps the biggest challenge with diversity is that it merely describes who is in the room. The goal that is generally stated is getting the right ratio or blend of people in the room. Rarely, if ever, does it begin to address how the people in the room interact with one another. Perhaps this is why the conversations and labels referring to the idea of diversity began to change as we moved through the decade of the 2000s. We had enough evidence to conclude that this is a very important initiative, but the topic had become cancerous because of the shortcomings of the many projects that were being implemented. Diversity initiatives lost their beauty and became known as lip service to the real issues.

Leading with Inclusion

As consultants, we searched for what was missing and began using a new term to describe what needed to be done: *inclusion*. As the use of this term became more widely accepted, we were free to express new goals—for example, make all members, partners, and employees feel welcomed and valued, not only for their abilities, but also for their unique qualities and perspectives. This message was definitely more positive, and everyone felt that he or she could get on board. The problem was that very little changed in terms of the implementation strategies. The goal was not really to give everyone these privileges, but rather to give them only to those who were members of a protected or disadvantaged class. Most of the people involved immediately noticed this flaw, but because it is not politically correct to mention it, we just kept going through the motions, with very little progress being made.

The legacy arc that takes us from acceptance to understanding is the place where the true journey toward celebrating diversity and including the value that everyone in the workspace contributes finally occurs. It causes us to reframe a critical argument. For some reason, we think that when we understand someone, we will accept that person. This may seem logical, but I would like to put forth the proposition that neither of these facets was ever meant to lead to the other. They are actually touch points on the continuum of inclusion, and understanding is definitely a more mature attribute than acceptance. In fact, I would like to argue that self-acceptance is the only form of acceptance that is truly necessary if we are to create a healthy and vibrant legacy. Because we are all free, we really don't have to accept anything else. We will always be free to choose who we want to be, what we like, whom we want to associate with, and what we want to do, but there will certainly be consequences that must be considered, especially in the work setting.

Acceptance, at its core, communicates the idea that we will somehow get to a place where we can receive favorably or even approve of something that we disagree with. When we express the challenge of agreeing with something that we disagree with, we are often encouraged to let it go. Can you see how one-sided this argument is? Is it any wonder that we always feel challenged by inclusion and diversity initiatives? Is there ever a time when we all can feel included and accepted for what we value? Must there always be an expectation that somebody must let go of what he or she values and believes in so that somebody else can feel accepted?

I do not believe that valuing the unique qualities and perspectives of others means that we must accept those qualities and perspectives.

I believe that when we take the time to understand those qualities and perspectives, it makes it easier for us to value them. In this case, "to value" actually means to regard something as important or of great worth. We can certainly do that without accepting it.

My first full experience with this concept came when I began working with Mitra. He was the first Buddhist I had had the privilege of working with. Naturally, as a Mormon, I was a bit concerned about how I might support him in his efforts, especially in his desire to connect his work to his spiritual values.

Since I had never personally studied the teachings of Buddha, I decided to read some things that would help me gain a better understanding of them. I asked him to recommend a couple of books, which he did, and I immediately purchased them and began the journey.

I was amazed at what happened next. Some of my Mormon friends were concerned that my search might lead me to renounce Mormonism, and more than one or two cautioned me straight out to be careful. Some of my friends from other faiths also wondered whether I might walk another path as a result of my study. Mitra encouraged me and assured me that there are many paths that lead to enlightenment. Fortunately, I never felt threatened by reading the materials he suggested.

I thought all of these responses were quite interesting. Why did nearly everyone I met think that the results of my study would necessarily lead to a conversion of some sort? Why didn't they think it was possible for me to simply read and enjoy the teachings without converting to or accepting what was being taught? The answer is quite simple: acceptance almost always requires us to convert. That is the very nature of that experience. To accept, we must let go.

I am thankful that my study of Buddhist teachings did what my friend Mitra suggested it would do. I felt enlightened. I saw things differently, and I was able to think about some things differently and to appreciate some things differently. To accept would have meant that I had to become a Buddhist. That would have been limiting and maybe even a little discouraging.

To understand meant that I could grow. I could learn new things that I could apply and use in my own way of being, but I didn't have to change my beliefs or my values in order to do so. Instead, I could add new understanding to the things I believed and valued. For example, one of the Buddhist values that I found to be most useful to me was the concept of mindfulness. That particular concept is explained by the teachings of Buddha in a very clear and precise way. It is a practice that would benefit any of us, and it is a practice that is not taught and explained as clearly in the Mormon faith. As I practiced mindfulness and came to understand how it works, I didn't become a Buddhist, I became a better Mormon. And that made me value the new understanding that I had gained even more.

This is the point of inclusion and diversity. It is being able to see and value the beauty that exists in alternative ways of being. I am convinced that in this practice, we must begin first with ourselves. Until we can accept what we believe and value, we will always be in a defensive position, and that will make it nearly impossible for us to understand what someone else believes or values.

Mitra taught me this lesson, too. In his work, he would regularly bring forward the beauties of Buddhism. While addressing the group, he would say something like, "I am a Buddhist, and in Buddhism we have this story or this belief that helps me in this way. . . ." The people in the room would think it was really neat. There seemed to be some magic about Buddhist ideas. They were different enough to attract attention without generating conflict. In some ways, it was hip to practice a Buddhist teaching.

In one of our private meetings, I told him that I was jealous of his freedom to do this. I said that there are a lot of beautiful teachings from my faith that I am unable to share. I told him that if I ever said something like, "I am a Mormon, and in Mormonism we have a story that teaches us this beauty . . . ," the people in the room would run for the doors, worrying that the missionaries might show up at their house.

Mitra laughed and told me that he thought this was my problem more than it was anybody else's problem. He challenged me to become more comfortable with my own faith, and to experiment with ways in which I could share the beauties of it with others without expecting them to be converted or to accept my way of thinking. I did, and I discovered that he was right. Once I accepted my own differences without worrying about whether or not somebody else would accept them, I was free to share my faith with others, and they were free to receive it in the spirit of understanding. My own level of comfort increased the comfort level of those around me, and no one ran for the door—at least not yet; are you still here? (smile)

Understanding truly is a higher value because it allows me to hold on to what I value most, while at the same time showing a sympathetic and at times even an energetic attitude toward another point of view.

To model this arc, I have used the most difficult example that I could personally think of—the expression of a religious belief. I want to be clear about something. The situation and circumstances I have just described are not unique to this one difference. The same is true for all the demographics that we typically use in the workplace, including race, religion, color, gender, national origin, disability, sexual orientation, age, education, geographic origin, and skill characteristics. We live in a diverse world, and when we learn to be inclusive, the culture we live in becomes much richer. When I have engaged with those who seem most different from me, I have learned many great things. This has never meant that I had to accept them, but when I have understood them, I have treated them with more kindness and more friendship. They have appreciated this, and never once have we struggled over what we can't accept about each other.

Key Leadership Lessons

Acceptance keeps us far away from the goals of inclusion. We should always treat others with respect, but that doesn't mean that we will accept everything about them. Neither you nor I should feel that we need to be accepted, because that would eventually mean that one of us would have to give up something that we value in order to be accepted.

When we pursue the goal of understanding others, we learn many fascinating things. Some of those things we will find useful, and others we will find not useful at all. Either way, we can appreciate the differences and even learn to celebrate the differences because when we learn through the eyes of understanding, we see how others truly value the differences that we cannot accept. The issue, then, must not be whether or not we can accept a menorah or a Christmas tree in a public place, but rather, whether or not we are willing to understand why that would be important to some of our fellow citizens. That is the real beauty of valuing someone else. We know we are there when we are no longer threatened by their differences.

When we move toward understanding on this legacy arc, we begin to create an energy and an environment around us that values the beliefs of others in a most beautiful way. No longer are we threatened with the concept of letting go of what we value so that we can fit in with what everyone else wants. There is much to be valued in this world, and when I understand that, I open up a space where others can come and be whole.

I want my legacy to include all of who I am. The only way I can do that is by understanding all of who you are, and then letting you comfortably share that with me. This value ultimately leads to the creation of a safe environment. No matter who you are, there is something of value that you can add to the circle of our contribution. There are many things about you and the other people in my sphere of influence that I am sure I will choose not to accept. If we decide to focus on our differences, we will always be at odds, and we will create an environment that promotes a lose-lose mentality. When we share our strengths with each other, taking the time to connect hope to hope, purpose to purpose, and dream to dream, we become focused on the great possibilities that brighten our collective future. We create this safety together by giving each other permission to share what we value, and by sharing what we value without the need to be accepted.

Leadership Questionnaire

How comfortable are you with your own values?

How willing are you to allow others to hold on to their own values, even those that are contrary to your own?

How willing are you to examine someone else's values?

How will understanding those values make you a better partner and coworker?

What work do you need to do on this legacy arc to become the person your legacy is calling you to become?

This legacy arc is truly one of my favorites. As I journey on it, I am reminded that if we were all the same, there would be no need for all of us. Understanding someone else is one of the most fascinating journeys we will ever undertake. It is a great gift that allows each of us to value others without letting go of what we value most. As soon as we open up to this reality, our legacy grows to a new level. Don't be afraid. There is room for both of us in this world.

Chapter 12

From Discussion to Dialogue

Discussion is impossible with someone who claims not to seek the truth, but already to possess it.

—Romain Rolland

I t is interesting to note the following things about the word *discussion*: it rhymes with concussion and percussion, the first synonym listed by *Webster's Dictionary* (http://www.merriam-webster.com/dictionary/discussion) is *argument*, and the first related word listed is *bull session*. Can you see a pattern emerging here? The original meaning of the word communicated the ideas of breaking apart, striking asunder, shaking up, examining, investigating, and asking for a judicial trial.

Even today, we understand that a discussion is a conversation that involves holding on to and defending our differences. This is a nice way of conducting an argument, but it is a terrible way of building a positive legacy. This is because it allows us to put the energy into the debate and focus the conversation on the positions that we agree or disagree with, instead of on the relationship that we wish to develop. These exchanges often result in failed communications that weaken our key relationships and shut down the creative expression of opinions.

The legacy arc that moves us from discussion to dialogue invites us to improve our relationships with others by openly engaging with them in a way that fosters meaningful communication. This legacy truly opens the doorway to vibrant communication.

The Greek word *dialogos*, which is the root of the English word *dialogue*, communicated the wonderful image of a flowing stream of consciousness that meanders among us, through us, and between us, making possible the emergence of new understanding. Rather than evoking an argument, this form of communication utilizes the power of inquiry to bring ideas to the surface, in the hope of creating a safe forum for all perceptions, even those that may be contrary to our own, so that they might also be valued.

A dialogue is different from a discussion. Instead of seeking resolution, and ultimately a winner, it provides an opportunity to explore the uncertainties that exist and the questions that are yet to be answered. This communication tool prepares us to think together so that we can use the energy of our differences as a way of arriving at collective wisdom.

Working in South America

The exciting work in Argentina that is described in the Preface provided me with a wonderful opportunity to work inside the arc that moves us from discussion to dialogue. When I arrived, there were several communication challenges that were seriously limiting the company's effectiveness. These rifts had created a major disconnect between the employee union and the management team.

It is important to realize that unions in South America are empowered to use fear and many other forms of destructive communication as a strategy to bring about the changes that they are struggling to create. There really are very few barriers that they must respect, and the law generally protects their right to threaten others. It is not uncommon for them to discover the home addresses of the management team and then form "mini mobs" that place derogatory billboards and handouts all over the neighborhoods where the managers that they are protesting live. They also position round-the-clock protestors that intimidate the managers and their families.

When I arrived in Argentina, a group of union representatives were positioned on the street in front of the organization that was employing me. They had a burning barrel, into which they periodically dropped some sort of minor explosive, kind of like a fireworks display. These explosions caused no damage, but their loud noise, amplified by the barrel, intimidated the workers and the management team and often delayed their entry into the building.

The president of operations asked me to work on this problem. We began by examining the union's complaints. Our hope was that we might find some common ground that could bring us together. We knew that we wouldn't be able to change everything, but we hoped that we could find something that we could offer as a starting point for a fruitful conversation. The current conversations were motivated only by fear and intimidation. For this reason, neither party could see anything more than the ground that it needed to protect. This meant that only win-lose scenarios were being proposed, which caused the attacks to continue. Neither of the parties could see a compromise. They could only envision the continuance of difficult conversations that would widen the gaps that separated the two parties.

As we examined the union's complaints, we realized that we did not understand the true issues behind each complaint. The first action we took was to invite the union leaders to an off-site meeting where they could informally communicate their complaints to us. We agreed as a team that we would only listen during this meeting, and we made it clear to the union representatives that we would offer no resistance or rebuttal. We just wanted to give them the opportunity to make their case calmly, without interruption. We agreed that many things needed to change, and we admitted that we didn't know what to do, or even what we *could* do to make things better.

The meeting was a success. The union representatives made their case in a calm and respectful way, and we asked the questions we needed to ask to gain greater understanding. At the end of the day, we had demonstrated our willingness to comprehend the problem. We requested a couple of weeks to consider all of their requests and scheduled a follow-up meeting.

We knew that we would never be able to honor all of their requests, but we didn't worry about that. Instead, we focused on the requests that we could honor, and then we prepared a detailed analysis of the scenarios that would have to occur for the other requests to be implemented. This meant that we did not say no to any of their requests. Instead, we offered the opportunity to collaborate on the solutions that would bring the more difficult requests to life.

In our second meeting, we invited the union representatives to meet us inside the company's offices. They had never been invited inside before. We brought them to the executive floor and treated them like partners and friends.

Naturally, they appreciated what we were willing to do, but were resistant to accepting what we stated that we could not do. They did not believe that we were telling them the truth about the situation. We offered more details, and we allowed them to ask more questions. The second meeting ended with a calm feeling of improving conditions. We did not reach agreement on any of the issues, but trust was building, and we scheduled several future meetings to continue our conversations. We asked for nothing in return. We simply wanted to create a safe environment where we could work on these issues together. Because we were so clear on what we could and could not do, we did not need them to agree with us. We just wanted them to continue to join us at the table.

The day after the second meeting, the protests in the neighborhoods of the executive team members were discontinued. The union representatives later told us that the openness of our meetings had caused them to see our leaders as people, and they were no longer willing to treat them like objects. A new respect was growing.

In our subsequent meetings, we reached many agreements that improved the employees' working conditions and strengthened the relationship between the management team and the union representatives. Naturally, we were unable to resolve all of the initial concerns. Both sides agreed that the circumstances required to resolve them would be too difficult to create. However, the gains we made in building trust made up for the differences that we were unable to overcome. Each party felt a commitment to building a better future. No one's ground was disrespected. Our dialogues had opened us up to each other and created a safe environment in which the issues could be examined. The work could go forward, even when we disagreed.

The impact that these conversations had on the productivity of the organization and the satisfaction of its union-represented employees was huge. The resolution of these issues made it possible for us to focus on other, more important issues. The increasing revenues created the possibility of further growth, led to many more opportunities to strengthen the relationship with the union, and made the organization's working conditions among the most favorable in its industry. What had once been a messy and challenging place to work became a workplace of choice. The company was able to attract the best employees. This progress happened quickly, and the organization continues to benefit from our efforts to this day. The company established a legacy of partnering with all of its stakeholders. This legacy was eventually extended to the government agencies, legal firms, and distributors who shared in the organization's success. As we brought all of these parties to the table and looked for ways in which we could better help each other, we created a vibrant network of respect and value.

Key Leadership Lessons

A dialogue is never focused on solutions. Instead, it provides the space for open communication involving the individual and the opposing challenges that each stakeholder must somehow overcome. In dialogue, a genuine effort is made to satisfy everyone's needs. This is the difference between attempting to forge win-win rather than win-lose solutions.

A dialogue is always focused on connecting the strengths of each party. A discussion is focused on finding the other's weakness. This distinction means that a dialogue brings us together as partners instead of enemies. It allows us to bring our best to the conversation, and it creates the opportunity for real growth solutions to emerge, instead of allowing the disputes that continue to separate the two parties to be the focus of our interactions.

Dialogue opens up communication; discussion often prevents it. The real difference is that instead of seeking the answers, we find ourselves asking the right questions. These questions allow us to examine all sides of the issue instead of simply holding on to our own ideas or defending our own position. We can't find what will work if we are willing to consider only what has worked in the past.

Dialogue requires us to actively listen to each partner in the conversation. While we may never be able to agree on everything, the simple courtesy of listening and understanding creates enough positive energy to move us forward in our efforts. When we listen, we begin to see what may be, and that prevents us from aggressively forcing an idea that will never be accepted. Our ability to listen inspires more collaboration than our ability to resolve the issues.

Finally, when we engage in dialogue, we are able to envision multiple solutions. In contrast, our discussion efforts are generally focused on finding the one best solution. Considering multiple solutions helps us to discover what will make things better for all of us. This may require us to stick with the dialogue well beyond our level of comfort, but it always results in a more powerful and long-lasting solution. The effectiveness of our decisions improves when we allow ourselves the time to carefully consider and ponder each option.

Naturally, there are times when we must favor discussion over dialogue. Hasty and urgent decisions require quick action, and we must know how to do that without having a major impact on the trust of those we lead. We must be willing to communicate that, although hasty decisions will always exist, we must do our best to ensure that they are the exception to the rule. Careful planning will help us to create the time and space we need to make decisions deliberately. Deliberate decisions afford the opportunity for us to engage our key stakeholders in fruitful dialogue. The more we demonstrate our willingness to do so, the greater our legacy will be.

Accordingly, this legacy arc not only influences our ability to communicate with others, but also influences the quality of the decisions that we make. You and I will be remembered both for our ability to foster beautiful dialogues and for the collaboration that we foster in the decision-making process, but that is not the most important contribution we make to our legacy as we work to move from discussion to dialogue. As we strive to engage in more open dialogue, we develop behaviors that help us to create greater levels of peace in our circles of influence, which in turn helps us to maximize the enjoyment we feel in our work-related experiences. Our greatest irritants are often the result of our inability to communicate effectively with others. The biggest hurts we feel and inflict upon others are also the outcomes of these failures.

The growth of our legacy is influenced by the lessons that we learn from others. The arc from discussion to dialogue accelerates the lessons that we learn because it provides us with many opportunities to listen to and learn from the experiences of others. Thoughtful and careful dialogue can help us to overcome any and all of our communication weaknesses.

Leadership Questionnaire

Here are some questions for you to consider before we examine the next arc.

What price do I pay when I am unwilling to open myself up to dialogue?

What activities are most effective in preparing me to suspend my judgments so that I can engage in open dialogue?

How can I foster the spirit of dialogue in others?

What are the decisions that I am facing right now that would benefit the most from a willingness to engage in open dialogue?

What can I do to make sure that dialogue happens more often?

Our legacy in the arc from discussion to dialogue is most influenced by our willingness to move to the center of the conversation and away from the sides. When we combine this with the lessons we learn from our journey on the arc that covers the ground between acceptance and understanding, we realize that we can move into the center without letting go of our identity. In fact, our identity, the very core that we are trying to defend when we engage in discussion, is actually strengthened as we move into dialogue. In this way, we actually use the energy of our differences to create solutions that never existed before. This helps us to develop greater common sense, thereby increasing our intelligence and our ability to lead others.

As we lead with this legacy arc in mind, we learn to gather our partners into intimate relationships that are full of trust. These relationships help us to take our conversations to the next level. As we seek to demonstrate our willingness to set aside our own opinions and suspend our own judgments, we communicate a willingness to make decisions that make things better for all parties. These experiences open us up to new possibilities, helping us to escape all forms of negative situations. Naturally, this increases our ability to respect and listen to others, while gaining strength and credibility in the use of our own voice. Ultimately, this frees us all to soar in ascending spirals.

Chapter 13

From Listening to Hearing

The art of conversation is the art of hearing as well as of being heard.

—WILLIAM HAZLITT

O ne of the most amazing truths that the people I work with must face is that others do not perceive them as being good listeners. This is especially difficult for senior leaders, who spend most of their time each day listening to the problems of their team members. They know that they must accept this feedback as reality, even though it does not match up with their personal perception of how things are. In their mind, listening is all they do every day.

For a very long time, these experiences caused me to single out listening skills as the most important leadership behavior to develop. I thought that if a person could improve and strengthen his or her ability to listen to others, that person's impact would be more valued by others. I was wrong.

I spent countless hours learning about the principles of positive listening. I enrolled in course after course that was focused on developing active listening skills, and I practiced those skills often. Then I trained many other leaders in these skills. The process itself was painful, and it required a lot of change, but the results were even more painful. Despite our best efforts, these leaders' key stakeholders noticed very little improvement. This only added to the frustration felt by those who truly wanted to grow.

Of all the legacy arcs, this may be the most counterintuitive. It definitely requires us to see things differently from the way we have been taught to see them.

It is quite probable that you have been taught to believe that hearing refers to the auditory sounds that your ear is able to perceive, while listening encompasses your ability to interpret the sounds you hear.

It is true that listening is an interpretive skill that requires us to not only pay attention to what is being said, but also be able to recognize how the story is being told, what words are being selected to tell it, how the person is using his or her voice, how the whole body is being used to communicate, and a plethora of other subtle and barely perceptible indicators that are being used to send the message. There is no doubt about it: listening is a complex, multifaceted skill that requires us to be just as attentive to what is being said as to what is not being said, and this taxes our patience as well as our skill set.

Together, all these steps are what make listening feel like an active process. It is true that we must actively pay attention, but beyond that, it becomes a passive process, for we can comply with these steps without ever taking further action. Listening requires us only to understand.

The words *hear*, *hearken*, and *heed* all stem from the same root word, which originally communicated the idea of attending to what is uttered with eagerness. To hear, we must actively and anxiously be willing to grant or comply with what is being requested of us. In a very real sense, our ability to hear demonstrates our willingness to obey, and this is precisely what makes it tough for us to do. Active hearing means that we are willing to do something about what is being said. Ultimately, that may requires us to put our own interests to the side while we make things better for somebody else. Remember, leadership is about making things better for others, and we can't do that until we are willing to subordinate our own self-interests for the good of the whole.

Betty's Leadership Story

It was through my work with Betty that I discovered the inner workings and intricacies that are represented by the critical arc that moves us from listening to hearing. When we began our work together, her listening skills received off-the-chart levels of dissatisfaction from her board, her peers, and her direct reports. They all knew that she was a bad listener, and they had told her so many times and in many different ways before they responded to our feedback instrument. They were honest in their evaluation, and their harsh ratings came as no surprise to Betty. In fact, she had predicted these results, and she freely admitted that her inability had been a source of frustration for her for many years. She confessed that she had made previous attempts to improve her skills, and although she had made some progress, the results were completely unsatisfying. She was more than ready to make listening the focus of our engagement, and she was hopeful that our efforts would finally help her to overcome this debilitating flaw.

In our initial conversations I noticed something rather remarkable. Betty was a good listener. She was skilled in the principles that are taught in most active listening courses. She was attentive, and she pleasantly demonstrated that she had an adequate understanding of what was being said in our conversations. Her proficiency in these skills actually fooled me for a while into believing that there was something wrong with her team. I thought that perhaps Betty's previous listening skills had been so bad that her team members were unable to recognize her progress. And so we began to discuss options for conducting an intervention that would help them recognize her improvement.

Of course, Betty was thrilled to receive my evaluation and readily agreed to put our plan in motion. It was only then that I discovered the real problem. Betty listened, but she never did anything with the information that she received. We would end each conversation with a list of follow-up steps. She never completed a single one. She just said that she had been too busy and that she would do better next time.

As the frequency of my interactions with her team members increased, I began to query them about her odd behavior. It was then that I discovered that the members of her team had not really rated her listening skills as much as they had rated her unwillingness to do anything about what they wanted from her. They knew that she had listened, and they even confirmed that she understood what they wanted, but she never took any proactive or corrective actions to make things better. This really frustrated her team members, and they didn't know what to do.

In my next meeting with Betty, we engaged in a very frank conversation. I did little to temper my approach. I shared my observations about our own interactions and the interactions she was having with members of her team. I asked her why she never did anything about what was asked of her, and she told me that she wanted to be a strong leader. Most of the people on her team were men, and she felt that if she always did what was asked of her, she would be seen as a weak woman. She felt that by not doing what was being asked of her, she would be able to maintain control of what was going on around her, and that would give her the ability to force others to do things her way. She was also concerned that if she created a conversation around the things that she didn't understand or didn't want to do, her team would discover that there were many things she didn't know, and that would cause her to lose credibility. There were many other reasons, but nearly all of them were connected to her desire to be seen as a strong leader. By some crazy train of thought, she felt that agreeing to take an action and then failing to take the agreed-upon action was a powerful way of establishing her authority. Naturally, this belief was seriously undermining her leadership image. Everybody was questioning her integrity and her fitness to lead.

We began immediately to work on some growth strategies. I asked her to make a few simple agreements that would guide our actions.

First, we agreed that she would never agree to take action on something that she had no intention of acting on. Until she was willing to take action, I invited her to commit to simply listening to her team members and promising them that she would take the time to think about what was being asked of her and consider the best options. This gave her the opportunity to develop a well-thought-out response.

Next, we agreed that in her follow-up meetings, she would commit to doing only what she was willing to do, and she would explain to the people involved why and how she had made her decision. This gave her the opportunity to demonstrate that she had considered the requests that they had made before she had made up her mind.

Finally we agreed that she would follow through on every commitment and that she would report her progress to all the stakeholders that were involved. This would help her to establish the trust she needed with her team.

Her actions had an immediate impact. The team experienced new levels of support from their leader, and in return, they were able to extend new levels of support to her. Betty discovered that when she thought about the things that were being asked of her before she made any decisions or commitments, then shared with her team how her decisions were informed and influenced by their suggestions and promptings, she was seen as a better listener. Most important, she was also seen as a better leader. Her team members reported that they had never expected her to do everything they wanted; they just wanted her to consider their ideas before she made a decision. For the first time, they felt as if they were in the loop and appreciated for their efforts. The dividends from taking these simple steps were huge.

Betty also experienced some unexpected personal growth. For the first time, she reported that she felt comfortable in her role. Before, she had always felt that she needed to hide her actions from the team. She had really felt that they would not want to follow her if she made decisions that were contrary to their requests, and this was why she made agreements without ever really intending to follow through. She didn't want her team members to discover that she didn't know everything. This behavior filled her full of doubt and made it impossible for her to establish herself as a trusted leader. Once she started communicating her actions to the members of her team and standing by her decisions, she felt a sense of empowerment that she had never felt before. She became more than a better listener. Her active hearing, demonstrated by her willingness to do something to make things better, inspired her team to make things better, too. Before, it had just seemed as if she was doing nothing about what was being communicated to her, and that was what made people think that she was a bad listener.

After my experience with Betty, I started to notice this same pattern with other leaders that I worked with. The leaders who took the time to understand what was being said, communicated the actions that they were willing to take, and then followed up on those actions, were seen as better listeners. I noticed that this was also true of those who were employed in supporting roles. When they demonstrated a willingness to act upon what they were told, the evaluation of their listening skills increased favorably.

This is the magic of this legacy arc. Hearing demands action, but that should never be interpreted as meaning that we must do everything that is asked of us. Our legacy is more dependent on the respectful way in which we respond to the requests that others make of us. No one ever really expects that anyone will do everything that he or she asks for. We just want to be heard.

Being heard is actually one of the "to bes" that we desire most. We want to make a contribution. We want to make a difference. We want to be involved in the decisions that affect our own work experience. We want to have a say, even when what we say is ultimately deemed to be unnecessary in the course that is selected. We want our voices to be heard before the decision is made.

Key Leadership Lessons

The people that we lead expect us to do something about what they say. They don't just want us to play back the words they said through the filter of our fancy active listening skills. They want us to make decisions and move forward.

They are not looking for us to incorporate every suggestion that they make. They simply want us to demonstrate that we considered their input before we made a decision. The more we indicate with our own words how much their input was valued, the more support we have for our decisions—even when we decide on something that is totally contrary to their ideas and suggestions.

Finally, hearing opens the way for dialogue because it implies a commitment to act. We must be careful to include all of our stakeholders in the process, or those on the fringe will feel that they don't matter. Our listening skills will help us to notice what is being said and what is not being said, and that will allow us to use our hearing skills to act appropriately. Remember, just because someone has not said anything to disagree does not mean that he or she has agreed. When we practice active hearing, we are comfortable with approaching our more silent team members privately, giving them the chance to share their thoughts and desires with us.

Our legacy is strengthened when we take action to make things better. Our actions demonstrate that we have either heard or not heard the requests that are being made of us.

Please consider these questions as you examine your movements on this legacy arc that takes us from listening to hearing.

Leadership Questionnaire

Do you take the time to consider what is actually being requested
of you?

How often do you nod your head when somebody else is talking? Do
you think this communicates something more than the simple fact
that you are listening to what that person is saying? Is it possible
that your head nodding is also communicating your agreement?

What do you do to ensure that you follow up on the agreements
you make?

What are the qualities of good listening that you admire?

How do you know when somebody is listening to you?

Who models good listening for you?

What actions are you willing to take to improve your active hearing
skills? How will you use these skills to communicate your
willingness to grant or comply with what is being asked of you?

There are many people who find the wisdom that we learn from this legacy arc to be contrary to what they have previously learned or accepted as being true. That does not change the truths that we discover as we move along the arc from listening to hearing. However, it does require us to once again suspend our own judgments so that we can experience what our legacy is calling us to be. Our legacy calls us to move beyond the simple interpretive nature of our listening skills and into the deeper actions that can come only by hearkening to what we have heard by granting the requests that others make of us and respecting their need to be heard. If you listen to the messages on this arc long enough, you will hear what I am saying and know that it is true. Let those who have ears hear this call.

Chapter 14

From Success to Significance

If A is a success in life, then A equals x plus y plus z. Work is x; y is play; and z is keeping your mouth shut.

—ALBERT EINSTEIN

I love this Albert Einstein quote because when we see success broken down into the simple variables that represent our daily actions, the results seem much less significant. I am sure that this is what he wanted to convey. Success is another figment of our imagination, yet for some reason, it is a chronic obsession that plagues us all. We crave the favorable outcomes. We hope and dream for prosperity in each and every venture that we undertake. Simply put, we want to succeed at everything that we do. Sometimes this desire is so strong that we wish for success at all costs, never pausing to consider how our success might affect those who are on our team.

I realize that we do our best to keep things in perspective, but this preoccupation with success and the pressure that we feel to be successful make it easy for many of us to put the wrong things first. When we are asked, we can define success in a hundred different ways. Most of us even have a list that dictates how we will measure it. These measures consider things like quality of life, time with our family, the opportunity to do what we do best every day, and happiness. Yet, whether we are willing to say it out loud or not, the real measure that most of us use is either making or having a lot of money.

Many people who are just trying to survive find it difficult to consider any of the other key indicators. Happiness doesn't put food on their table. But our obsession with money becomes a nonissue when we are faced with a life-threatening crisis. Suddenly, our money, the things we can buy with our money, and the stuff we have become meaningless. I say that they become meaningless, but you and I know that they have always been meaningless. We can't buy what we really want with money. We can use it to improve our quality of life, but those who use money to define their success are usually the most tired, stressed, and miserable people I know.

Naturally, this way of thinking creates a conflict when we go to work each day. Our success on the job is recognized and rewarded in dollars and cents. We get paid for what we do, and the amount that we get paid communicates to others, whether we like it or not, how successful they think we are. Money fools us into being comfortable, but the comfort that we feel is only temporary. Eventually, we all must face the fact that a life that is defined by possessions and profession is shallow and insignificant.

The legacy arc that charts the inventure from success to significance helps us to remember to lead with our long-term values instead of our short-term hungers. We know that we can't take our money with us when we pass on. This reminder also helps us to focus on creating significance in and through our work-related experiences, not just an admirable net worth.

Blair's Story

My best friend Blair helps me to keep these things in perspective. We met on the job when we were both telemarketers. We worked for a company that was selling success during the time when telemarketing was new, and people were still willing to answer the phone and listen to what was being offered. We were the company's top salesmen, and we battled each week to outdo the other. We enjoyed a healthy competition that pushed each of us to do our best. We made a lot of money, especially for a couple of young men in their very early twenties.

During our free time, we would share our goals for success and dream about what life would be like. Blair wanted to be a big-shot attorney. He was pursuing that goal at a local university. I was still figuring out what I wanted to do, and so we raised the possibility of opening a law firm together. He was a year older and much wiser than I, so I listened to him and learned from his plans.

At the end of one summer, we both got married and decided that it was time to move on from the field of telemarketing. Neither of us had ever thought of telemarketing as a career. It was just a job to get us through school. Inserting Katie and Stacy into our relationship strengthened our friendship, and we became more like a family than like a couple of guys who had met at work. Though we moved away from each other to pursue our own successes, we were always connecting the dots of our lives together.

One day, Blair called me and told me that he was no longer interested in becoming an attorney. I can't remember exactly how he said it, but he said that he had decided to pursue something that fascinated him even more than law: he had decided to become a seminary teacher. I really didn't know what to say. As telemarketers, we had made more money in a month than the starting salary that he would receive for a year. I asked him how Katie felt about his decision—after all, she had married him on the assumption that he would be a lawyer. He said that she supported his decision, and that they had put the proper plans in place to ensure that they would have enough money to meet their needs. I wondered how he would ever make enough money to live out his dreams and his aspirations.

Twenty-five years have now passed since he made that decision. Our relationship continues, tested by late-night arguments around a card table, but strengthened by knowing that we are always there for each other. During this time, I have watched with great interest as these dear friends have grown and developed their talents. Both are now respected and highly regarded authors. Their calendars are filled with speaking opportunities. Blair still teaches in his church's educational system, and Katie works on her projects from home so that she can be there to raise their own seven children. Despite the income limitations of his profession, I have never seen them lack for what they needed. They have enjoyed sufficient financial resources to meet their needs. They live in a house that is big enough for their family. They drive cars that are big enough and reliable enough for them to get where they need to go together. They are well dressed and well fed. They have everything that they need. They are happy.

So Blair never became an attorney. Instead of living into success, he decided to live into significance. Over the years, I have met many people who live in and around the town where Blair and Katie live. When I ask them if they know my friends, the answer is always a resounding yes, and then they tell me stories of the impact that Blair and Katie have made on their life. I have also met many of Blair's students, who are equally inspired. I am not sure about the number of students that have passed through his classes, but there are many who know and respect Brother Blair for the things he taught them about life.

Blair uses his time, his talents, and his energy to create a work experience that allows him to live into significance, not instead of success, but in addition to the many successes that he continues to enjoy. He built a reputation and a career in an area that best matches his talents, and this gives him the opportunity to have an impact on many people each and every day. His contributions as a lawyer would have been far less significant. I admire the courage and the wisdom he demonstrated, while still a very young man, to figure these things out.

I am interested by the question, "What really allowed Blair to create significance?" Do you think he was able to do so simply because of the profession he selected? Do our professions really determine whether or not we can shift our focus from success to significance? I personally think that our professional interests contribute only a very small portion to our legacy of significance.

Significance, like nearly all the facets on the right-hand side of the legacy arcs, requires us to value the qualities more than the quantities. Significance is the quality of being important. Your level of importance is not measured by how many people in the world have heard of you. It doesn't matter how many followers you have on Twitter. Instead, it is measured by how the people closest to you have benefited from your impact. Your significance is measured by the consequences of your actions. At work, your professional footprint can be valued only when you are consciously contributing your best, regardless of whether or not you ever gain any additional value. If you are constantly working to make things better, your level of significance will increase. If you are constantly complaining and draining the energy in your work environment, then you will always be just an insignificant irritant to your coworkers, no matter how much money you make.

Even when we define success as happiness and seek after it, we miss the mark. Leo Rosten, the acclaimed author and humorist, once said, "I cannot believe that the purpose of life is to be happy. I think the purpose of life is to be useful, to be responsible, to be compassionate. It is, above all, to matter, to count, to stand for something, to have made some difference that you lived at all." This is significance. We create it by stepping in and filling someone else's need. This is what separates success from significance. Success is almost always a selfish pursuit, while significance is always gained through selfless service. Compared to significance, the bright lights of success fade quickly.

The time that we spend on this arc creating success is often wasted because almost everyone finds it unfulfilling. It doesn't matter where you are working now; you have the power to create significance. Remember, you are going to be there more than anywhere else, so your workplace is actually the best place for you to seek significance. Here are a couple of ideas to help you in your efforts.

Sooner or later, your job will end. Either you will retire from work altogether, or you will move on to a new place of employment. When we put this truth into proper perspective, we are able to help others without having a personal agenda. After all, what difference does our personal agenda make when we are no longer there? It is never too early in your career to start thinking about your legacy of significance. Ask yourself, what do you really want to contribute to your organization before you retire or move on? How do you want the people there to remember you?

When you consider how you want your coworkers to remember you, you connect yourself with the importance of authentically showing up to work each day with one thought in mind: "How can I make things better around here?" It is amazing how infectious the attitude of making things better is to those who work with us. Once we demonstrate our commitment, others feel free to copy us.

The focus on making things better always reminds us to think about the work experiences that the people around us are having. Do you think it is possible to be constantly preoccupied with your next raise or promotion and still be thinking about how you can help the people you work with? These types of thoughts usually put you into competition with others instead of into service to others. Your value to your organization will be significant when you can genuinely demonstrate that you care about the people you work with.

Your legacy of significance will also grow when you take the time to help people who are farther down on the corporate ladder. Your willingness to mentor and support others yields amazing benefits long after you are gone. You don't ask how you can help, because you already know. You were once where they are now, so just remember how you felt and offer to help them overcome the challenges that they are facing.

We will talk more about service in a later chapter, but it is worth mentioning here that your talents and energy are needed in other organizations, too. As you share your talents in other spaces and places, your legacy of significance increases. Service is one of the best accelerators that move us from success to significance. Just look around. It won't take you very long to discover a place where you are needed.

When you are serving others, you will discover a secret about significance: it really is your choice. You get to decide how deeply others will feel your impact. The earlier you make this choice, the more connected your significance will be to your success.

Another secret about significance is that the more we learn to temper our wants, the more freedom we have to leave behind the stressful reach for success. The simple life still inspires us to work hard. The real difference is the pressure we feel while we are working. When we live with fewer expenses, we can share our resources more freely. This includes our time and our financial resources.

Finally, our reach for significance is always enhanced when we learn about how other people have lived to create their own significance. There are many autobiographies and biographies in the world. We just need to decide if we want to learn about the life of SpongeBob SquarePants or Mohandas Gandhi. It will always be our choice, and the information that we put into our brain will help give us many ideas on how we can create significance.

Key Leadership Lessons

Finally, here are some of the key lessons that I learned from watching my friend Blair create significance in his life and in the lives of others.

The first one is quite simple. Your legacy of significance will always be around longer than you will be around. We all know people who are still mentioned at the watercooler, even though they haven't been around for a very long time.

Second, significance has a life of its own. Your impact will inspire someone else to make an impact, and that person will make that impact on the life of someone else. It is a never-ending gift. Nothing can stop it once it starts rolling.

Finally, significance satisfies our deepest aspirations. No matter how hard we try, success will never be able to do that for us.

When you go to bed this evening, spend some time thinking about the choices you made today to create significance and consider these questions.

Leadership Questionnaire

If you got a better job today and moved away tomorrow, what would people say about you at the watercooler when you were gone? How will you be remembered at work?

If you took a new job and discovered that a previous coworker or boss was also working at your new company, would that person be happy to see you?

It is your time that you are spending at work each day. You get to choose how you will show up each day. The way you do that says a lot about what you value most. Let significance be the primary guide for all of your legacy-making efforts. Work to make things better for others, and everything else will fall into place.

Chapter 15

From Ambition to Meaning

Ambition is so powerful a passion in the human breast, that
however high we reach we are never satisfied.

—HENRY WADSWORTH LONGFELLOW

A t first glance, the arc from ambition to meaning looks remarkably similar to the arc from success to significance. However, upon closer inspection, we begin to see the major distinctions. Significance is the mark that we leave behind when we are no longer here, whereas meaning is the personal fulfillment that is ours to enjoy as we develop and grow through our own experiences.

Our daily work can be as full or as devoid of meaning as we choose to make it. It is our personal responsibility to determine the activities that will create either authentic reality or disappointing illusion. Our focused efforts take us deeper into the existential nature of the total person.

In the early part of our career, we are driven by our ambitions. We are eager to prove our worth to others, so we labor to achieve recognition, often without regard for the sacrifices we are making. We know

149

that we need to be seen so that we can be promoted. We are willing to work hard because there is an unwritten psychological contract at work that promises something that we all want: increased responsibility. This eventually leads to more free time. We work to get ahead so that we can stop and smell the roses later.

The problem is that the promise of free time is one of the many work-related mirages that leave us filling thirsty and unfulfilled. Ambition can never be satisfied. As long as it is allowed to guide our legacy-making efforts, it will continually confuse us as we work to find the meaning in our daily efforts. When we make the shift from ambition to meaning, we let our authentic self be our guide. We pause and reflect so that we can better understand the nature of our work and the value that we derive from it. We seek to understand the relationships between what we really want and what we are getting, and then we embark on the path that allows us to contribute in the most meaningful ways.

Ambition necessarily propels us forward during the early stages of our careers, but we must allow meaning to take over as we wind down our work experiences, or we will be endlessly frustrated. This is because at some point, before we reach the end of our careers, we will gain our last promotion, receive our last raise, and be asked to lead our final project. After that, we may be seen only as a valuable contributor, which means that our reward will be to do a lot of work that nobody else is qualified to do. This is why we must make sure that we allow meaning to guide our work experiences.

Strategic Leadership

I was hired by a public utility company to create a strategic management plan for its customer service department. The company had just received the data from its customer satisfaction survey, and for the fifth year in a row, its ratings had declined. The employees in the customer care center were discouraged by this report, and many of them were struggling to be engaged.

The scope of my work included the creation of an overall strategy as well as very specific employee and customer engagement strategies. Bob, a 40-year employee of the PUC, was the internal lead, and we were assigned to shape and craft the plan together.

To be honest, Bob was overqualified for the job. During the course of his career, he had managed some of the most demanding projects and led the most important divisions. Now he was relegated to being a one-man show in a project with boundaries and objectives that were poorly defined. The purpose of the project was declared to be important, but the resources committed to its success were minimal. There were whispers that the company had created this project specifically for Bob. It wanted to remove him from active duty without forcing him to retire. Many people saw the project as a box to contain him in while he prepared for his retirement. But Bob was not ready to retire. He was only 62 years old when the project began, and he was planning on working at least another three years before he took the last carpool home.

The funding for the project would last only six months. All of Bob's normal responsibilities had been assigned to somebody else when he agreed to be the lead on this project. He had been told that this was necessary so that he could focus all of his efforts on the project. This meant that upon completion of the assignment, he would have no place to go in the organization. As we began our work together, it was clear that Bob was feeling that the company had really pulled the rug out from under him. He was bitter and unfocused. While we worked, he often voiced the observation that he had spent his life in the service of his organization, and now, as he neared the end of his career, it seemed as if it was coldly exchanging him for a newer model. I did my best to keep him focused on our work.

The project required us to spend a lot of time together thinking about the actions that we would need to take in order to create the success we envisioned. During our breaks, I would ask Bob to share with me the history of his work with the company. The details were fascinating. The company was celebrating 60 years in existence, and Bob had been involved in many of the efforts that had helped it grow to its current level. As we discussed his hopes for the future, it was clear that he was having a hard time shaking the feeling that the company had let him down. He really didn't know what he was going to do when the project ended, but he knew that the company's culture would allow him to hide in some forgotten corner for the next three years while he waited to retire. He didn't want to just collect a paycheck, but he really couldn't see any other options.

One day, I was summoned to the CEO's office. She began our conversation by reminiscing about some of the other assignments that I had facilitated for the company, and then she asked me to accept a special assignment on her behalf.

The effects of the economic recession were finally catching up to the PUC, and it was staring some very difficult but necessary budget cuts in the face. The company needed to reduce its headcount, something that it had never done before. The CEO was worried about the impact that this would have on the company's culture, and so she was hoping that the company could entice some of its older employees to retire early. She knew that if this strategy failed, then some very difficult decisions would have to be made that would disrupt the goodwill that the firm was working hard to preserve. She asked me if I would facilitate the early retirement conversations with a list of employees that the company had identified as most likely to accept the offer. As I perused the list, I noticed Bob's name, and it was only then that I began to feel the personal impact of the difficult conversations that I was about to have. Because I was well acquainted with Bob's hopes for the future, I began to imagine similar hopes for each person on the list. Each of them would be offered a fair package, but most of them were working for more than money. These employees were some of the longest tenured, and their work was an important part of their life.

I reluctantly accepted the assignment and decided to begin with Bob. For a couple of days, I tested the waters by asking him about his future plans. We were more than halfway done with the strategic management project, so it was natural for us to discuss what he thought he would be doing when we were finished. He continued to hold on to the belief that he would either be assigned to a new project or simply find a struggling work group that he could support. Nothing he said suggested that he had even considered retiring before he was 65.

I had discovered through our many conversations that he had spent some time working with the chief financial officer. The impact of the recession on the PUC was well documented. There were regular stories in the local paper that discussed the losses that utility companies were experiencing as a result of there being fewer utility customers because of the high number of vacant homes and of financially strapped homeowners who were wisely managing their use of power, gas, and water to save money. One day I brought this up and asked him what he thought his company would do to protect its profit margins. Without hesitation, he said, "I suppose they will have to start letting people go." This surprised me, because it was a strategy that municipalities rarely employed.

It was then that I turned the conversation to his personal circumstances. I asked him if he had considered retiring early, and he said no. I enjoy being direct, so I informed him of the assignment that his CEO had given me. As we discussed my assignment, I told him that he had two options: Option A, he could negotiate an early retirement package, or Option B, he could wait until the organization let him go. When he wondered why I thought the organization would let him go, I asked him to consider whom he would let go: somebody who was finishing a temporary assignment and did not have a future role, or somebody who had a current role. He understood my point, but he was too stubborn to accept the fact that this could somehow affect him. He was more than stubborn; he was very angry that I would even bring it up, and even angrier that the organization would think that it could just cast him aside. I asked him to think about it, and to discuss it with his wife that evening after work. I invited him to consider what he would do with the next three years if he could do anything he wanted to do.

When I saw him next, there was a new light in his eyes. He told me that he had accepted the idea of retiring early, and then he thanked me for asking him to think about how he wanted to spend the next three years. He said that when he had left the night before, he had been quite certain that he would be able to force the company to keep him until he was ready to retire. He dreamed up age discrimination complaints and lawsuits and knew that he would be safe, but then he started thinking about how all of that would affect his work. He had enjoyed his work, and he knew that this approach would cancel out all of that enjoyment. For the first time, he considered working somewhere else, and just the thought of doing that made him feel free—and he was free, because he was going to have his retirement income, and for the first time in his life he would be able to do whatever it was that he wanted to do.

He knew of several places that would value his engineering and project management skills, and that made him feel very confident that he would be able to find another job. However, instead of focusing on those opportunities, he began to think about all the possibilities that would be available to him.

He had originally planned that when he retired at 65, he would sell his home and move to a neighboring state so that he could work for a charitable foundation. He realized that there was nothing preventing him from doing that now, and the thought of doing so helped him see that this would be a much more meaningful use of the next three years. By the time he arrived at work, he had already scouted out a couple of properties that would meet his needs. He could feel the energy that was growing with each step. For the first time in a long time, he was alive. Once again, he was in charge of his destiny.

I am quite certain that under different circumstances, Bob could have found meaningful work with his lifetime employer. Each of us can do that, even when we feel as if we are in a dead-end job. But in order to do that, we must be willing to ask the question, "What would I do, if I could do anything I wanted to do?" We actually have that choice. We can work anywhere we want to work, and this is why we are responsible for making the meaning in our own work experiences.

Key Leadership Lessons

I learned many lessons about making meaning as I worked with Bob. Here are some of the most valuable.

First, the pressure of providing for our needs makes it easy for us to believe that the reality that we are experiencing is the only possible reality. This causes us to go to work each day, even when we know that we should be looking for another opportunity.

Second, until we examine all of the alternative possibilities, it is very difficult for us to make meaning. Without this evaluation, we have no way of knowing what is meaningful.

Third, even though Bob pursued an opportunity that was beyond the boundaries of his workplace, making meaning does not require this. In any organization, there will always be multiple roles that we can fill. Some of those roles will be more meaningful than others. It is our responsibility to pursue those more meaningful roles and get ourselves in position. The organization will not do this for us.

Finally, the fear that often prevents us from looking around and engaging in more meaningful roles is quickly replaced by the energy we feel when we shift our focus from ambition to meaning. This energy is life-changing, and it has the power to add life to our years. Most of the time, we are already working in the right field; we just need to move around in our role. When we do that, we find the meaning that we have been seeking.

Every career will include a few meaningless years. We should not be worried about this. Instead, we must listen to our own voice. It will tell us when we are out of tune with our purpose and meaning. Then it will help us identify the roles and responsibilities that would provide us with the opportunity to live up to our purpose and create more meaning.

Until we get this clear, we will spend most of our lifetime simply working for the weekend. What a horrible waste of the 117,000 hours that we will spend at work. I feel that they can be so much more meaningful than that. We work so that we can learn and grow. When we allow this purpose to guide our work experiences, then we find ourselves engaging in more meaningful work.

Meaningful work can scare us because it requires more from us. Sometimes we stay at a place too long, and other times we move on too quickly just to avoid stepping up to the next level. The following questions will help you determine your next steps. May they, and the other questions that they evoke, help you bring your most meaningful work into focus.

Leadership Questionnaire

What am I learning at work? What evidence is there that I am
   growing?
Do I feel engaged by my efforts?

If I were three years away from retirement, how would I want to
    spend my time?
What are some of the other ways that I could provide for my needs?
    Do any of these alternatives seem more meaningful to me?

Sometimes the meaning is much simpler than we expect. Please don't
be surprised or disappointed if your examination of your journey on the
arc from ambition to meaning only brings into focus the reality that you
are already deriving a lot of meaning from your daily work experiences.
Sometimes we take what is so near to us for granted. Instead of skipping
on to the next chapter, please take a moment to capture the gratitude you
feel at being so engaged. Doing so will increase your sense of awareness
and sharpen your resolve to make more meaning each day. Who could
ask for anything more than that?

Chapter 16

From Growing Older to Growing Whole

A twenty-three-year-long study in Ohio determined that people who saw growing older as something positive lived a whopping seven and a half years longer than those who didn't.

—Victoria Moran

Eventually, we all reach a point when we are either unwilling or unable to work. When we think about our retirement from the workforce, most of us hope for the opportunity to exit on our own terms. We want to be healthy when we retire. We want to have saved and invested wisely enough so that we can live happily for all the rest of our days. We want to be able to enjoy it all with someone we love. We want to continue making contributions to our circle of influence. We want to live.

As we think about accomplishing all of these objectives, we might also dream of having a deep tan and a low handicap. No matter what it is that we plan on doing, we promise ourselves that we will never again spend more time working than living. We envision a carefree life that is full of purpose and meaning and devoid of stress and anguish.

Unfortunately, this picture proves to be contrary to reality. In fact, a recent poll conducted by the Harvard School of Public Health that included 1,254 retired individuals found that 75 percent of those surveyed believed either that life in retirement is worse than their life was before they retired, or that the overall quality of life they are experiencing in retirement is about the same as it was when they were working full time. This is an important result for us to consider, because it clearly demonstrates that the purposes we meet through our work and the opportunity to be productive each day contribute significantly to our ability to be satisfied with the life we live.

What Is Retirement?

Too often, we look at retirement as the day when we no longer have to work, only to discover that most of us really enjoy working. Our work educates us, and it provides us with many opportunities to learn and to grow. It gives structure and contrast to our life and helps us to stay connected to a vibrant social network. There is no doubt that our legacy would be reduced without the contributions of our employment history.

The goal of retirement, then, must not be to stop working, but rather to find work that continues to inspire our personal growth. It is quite possible that this work will be the continuation of our career, not the end of it. But retirement might also provide us with the freedom to use our individual talents and strengths in ways that were previously unavailable to us. Whatever we do, it must be of our own choosing. We must use the autonomy that retirement gives us wisely. We can no longer be slaves to our work.

As we explore the arc that moves us from growing older to growing whole, we experience an epiphany that helps us to see that the goal of work is not to create success and security. Instead, our work must be the vehicle for connecting us to purpose and meaning. Without it, we simply find ourselves lollygagging around in boredom. We need work to keep us moving forward. It connects us to a bright future.

This is especially important for us to remember as we age. The idea of growing older concerns most of us because it fills our mind with visions of what we are going to lose. Age has a funny a way of doing that. The ideas associated with aging are closely connected to the ideas associated with entropy, which means an inevitable and steady deterioration. We get old, we get sick, and then we die. That is the path that we all must eventually walk. None of us is anxious to get in line for that.

Consequently, most of the societal messages that we receive encourage us to hang on to our youth at all costs. Just think about some of our aging celebrities and everything they do to maintain their youthful looks. Some of them have worked so hard at it that we barely even recognize them when we see them. They may look young, but they don't look anything like they did when they were young. Most of us agree that there are some things that get better with age, but we have a hard time believing that people do.

Naturally, we do experience losses when we age, and ultimately one of those losses will be life; no one gets out alive. If we choose to make these losses the focus of our energy, then we will grow old, tired, irritable, and useless. I think the idea of being useless is really our biggest fear. We want to add value. Society sometimes communicates to those in our elderly population that the older they get, the less value they have to offer. We must not believe that message. As we grow older, we have many things to offer to our circle of influence.

This legacy arc encourages us to consider what it means to grow whole. It gives us a chance to think about all of the parts that make us who we are, and then the opportunity to figure out how we can use our wholeness to influence others. When we focus on growing whole, we look to the future instead of the past. As we look, we see the spaces and places where the total person that we have become might continue to contribute to the greater good. We also see how we can continue to grow and develop. This means that instead of living a life that is defined by our entropy, we can see that we are remembered for our recurring blooms of inspiration.

Wholeness is guided by the future. There is always an opportunity to be inspired by what we see on the road ahead, and that gives us permission to work on our legacy with more freedom and energy than we have ever had before.

As we spend time in this legacy arc, we form a synergy among all the other legacy arcs. It is in this space that we learn how to bring together our new purposes, our continued opportunities to grow, our most powerful aspirations, our trained focus, our enlightened understanding, our increased ability to engage others in dialogue, our willingness to act on what we hear, our desire to create significance, and our search for meaning into one great legacy-making inventure. This is the time for us to become a total person. We have spent years during our careers waiting for this day. A commitment to growing whole keeps us reaching for a bright and beautiful future.

When Peter Drucker passed away, he was nearly 96 years old. At the time of his death, Jack Welch called him "the greatest management thinker of the last century." As I think about that comment, I often wonder, how did Peter Drucker remain relevant for so long? What was it about him that allowed him to continue to build his legacy long after he had formally left his work responsibilities?

The answer is that he never stopped working. He continued to contribute in both new and familiar ways. In fact, I know someone who visited Peter just two weeks before he died. He told me that even though Peter's health was failing, he still took the time to have a lively discussion about the state of the world and the future that we all face. Even when he was nearing death, his awareness of what was going on in the world, his hope for the future, his deep insight, and his continuous commitment to his own purpose of helping others achieve their goals was being vibrantly carried out. There is a rumor that he even answered phone calls on the day of his death. How did he continue to build his legacy? By continuing to be active in the work that he loved.

For some of you, retirement is still many years away. Others of you may be nearing the end of your careers right now. Still others of you are already comfortably living in retirement. It doesn't matter where you are; there is still time for you to consider what you must do to grow whole. Tucked into the concept of growing whole is the reality that retirement must not be a withdrawal from doing what we do best. Instead, it must be a time management exercise. Since it won't be long before all that is left of us is the memory of our legacy, we must be anxiously engaged each day in living out our purpose. This is how we make meaning. We stare into the face of possibility, and we discern how we can make what we see a reality. Our days in retirement must be so much more than the opportunity to stay up late, sleep in late, and sit in an easy chair all day long. If that is all we do, the remainder of our days will be a long, slow, and boring process.

When we stay connected to our future, there is always something to live for, there is always more that we can give, and there is always someone we can help. Those who see this possibility are the ones who continue to inspire.

Think about the people you know who either are approaching retirement or have already left the workforce and are now in retirement. I am sure that in your network, there are at least two kinds of people: those who are happy and enjoying life, and those who are miserable and ready to check out. What is it that makes the same experience so different? Why are some people happy and others miserable?

Now take some time to think only about the ones who are happy. You know, the ones whom you want to be like when you grow up. When was the last time you sat down to visit with them? Have you ever asked them what they are doing to stay focused? Have you asked them for their advice on how you can most effectively live out the experiences that are ahead of you? There are many lessons that elderly people can teach us. Are we wise enough to seek out those lessons? I certainly hope so.

I work with a lot of people who are in the second half of their lives. As a result, I spend most of my time learning about what it really means to lead with our legacy in mind. I am certain that legacy making is the most important work we will ever do. It is a work from which we will never want to retire. There are many surprises in this great work. Here are some of my favorites about growing whole.

Key Leadership Lessons

When we are young, we feel indestructible. We may not always be confident of our abilities, but we somehow believe that we are strong enough to survive any circumstances. As we get older, the threat of sickness and death becomes more and more real. Our increased awareness of this reality makes us afraid and causes us to think that we might not have enough in the future. Our fear leads us to take fewer risks. Growing whole is a risky business. Sometimes we just have to say what the heck, so that we can move beyond our fear. When we do, we discover that our perceptions of work and life are inventions of our own mind. When we finally see that, we are finally free to enjoy life. Don't wait too long to let go of fear. It will never do you any good. Just let go.

Second, when we are young, we think we know it all. The arc from growing older to growing whole teaches us that there is always something to learn. As we age, it is difficult to let go of the confidence we feel when we allow ourselves to believe that we know everything, but we must let go of that, too. There are things that people who are 20 years older know, but that you and I are not ready to understand. This is because we have not had the experiences that we need in order to be able to comprehend the intelligence they have gained. When you talk with elderly people about what they have learned, make sure that you either record this experience or get them to write down what they have learned in their own hand. This practice has two important purposes. First, it demonstrates to the person you admire that you value his or her wisdom. Second, it gives you a record to go back to when you reach the same age. When that time arrives, you will be pleasantly surprised to discover how much you were unable to comprehend when you heard it the first time, and how valuable it is for you to revisit the wisdom of your friend as a peer. Writing things in our own hand, recording our voices and images, and saving our important work in a digital file are all part of our legacy-making efforts. When we allow our wise elders to contribute to the file, we increase the depth of what we leave behind and of what we take with us.

Finally, you may have noticed that in both of these key lessons, I mention the idea of letting go. Growing whole is an exercise in letting go of many things. When I say that it is important to let go, I do not wish to imply that we must forget. Letting go is not an exercise in forgetting; it is an exercise in remembering. When we let go, we begin to authentically learn about who we really are, and we remember how to behave. When we let go of the stumbling blocks that prevent us from moving forward, the ground is cleared for our legacy to bloom. The circumstances no longer dictate our actions. Instead, we become prepared to create the circumstances in which we will act.

Our legacy is an outcome of our actions. We can either act or be acted upon. It is our choice, but it is only our actions that keep us moving forward.

Leadership Questionnaire

How are you using your work and life experiences to help you become
a total person?

What is it about your work that you enjoy and wish to continue doing
after you retire?

How will you create the opportunities to continue doing what you
do best?

How will you ensure that you use your time wisely?

As I finish writing the end of this chapter, I naturally find myself thinking about the time when my own life will end. There are many people who avoid this line of thinking. I find it to be rather exhilarating, not because I want to die, but because I want to live. I know that if I think about my future, I can look forward with many aspirations. I see the end as a finish-line experience. It is a time of great celebration. Seeing it this way helps me prepare by becoming the person I want to be and doing the things I need to do to become that person right now. Although I cannot predict when I will cross the finish line, I am responsible for how I will cross. This is why I know that I will never retire. Instead, I will be active in doing many good things of my own choosing. In a sense, you can say that I retired a long time ago — not from my work, but from the false expectations that come from focusing on the wrong things. Because I am thinking about growing whole, I am living a well-spent life. This means that my work is aligned with my purpose.

The legacy arcs in this section are designed to help you on the journey toward thinking about the right things. I want to cross the finish line like Peter Drucker—peacefully in my sleep after enjoying a beautiful and meaningful career. That takes work!

PART III

The Seasons of Leadership

Chapter 17

Follow, Lead, and Serve

Nature does nothing uselessly.

—ARISTOTLE

Are leaders born or developed? Obviously, this question has the potential to draw us into the age-old debate on nature versus nurture, which has puzzled some of the greatest philosophical and psychological minds for centuries. I do not wish us to be mired in this debate. There seems to be enough evidence to conclude that there are both natural and socialized influences that contribute to our personal and professional development opportunities. Instead, I want you to consider your individual responsibility for managing both of these factors as you seek to lead with your legacy in mind.

The legacy arcs that are presented in Chapters 7 through 16 represent some of the nurturing behaviors that guide us on this quest. It is now time for us to turn our attention to the environmental conditions and circumstances that also affect our legacy-making efforts.

Because you are free to choose the places where you spend your time working, it is important for you to realize that on this shared journey, any conversation about the influence of your organization's specific environment and culture on your professional legacy would be counterproductive. Naturally, your workplace environment significantly influences your efforts, but by virtue of your employment contract, you have already accepted those conditions. If you find them to be too harsh or too limiting, then it may be time for you to seek other employment. You are responsible for examining your unique set of circumstances frequently.

Accordingly, we turn our attention away from the specific circumstances found in your individual work experiences and toward the general environmental patterns that frame all of our opportunities to make things better.

It may be helpful to liken these conditions to the familiar four seasons that define the calendar year. This gives us a model that illustrates a cycle of seasonal growth defined by unpredictability. Therefore, let us allow springtime to represent our followership opportunities. This season is the most favorable time for our early growth and development. The summertime of our work experiences represents the formal leadership roles and opportunities that are assigned to us. It is during this season of our career that we normally mature through capital "L" leadership experiences. The fall is a season of slowing growth. It is the time to harvest. The fruits of the harvest are gathered and stored for sustaining purposes. The fall of our career provides us with opportunities to share our yield with others through carefully selected acts of service. Finally, the winter is a dormant period that represents either a time of renewal or our complete retirement from our labors. Each of these seasons provides us with opportunities to live out our goal of making things better for others. They are very different seasons, and they provide us with significantly different benefits. In Chapters 18 through 20, we will examine the environments of followership, leadership, and service.

These seasons of leadership, like any environmental system, significantly change as time passes. As they change, we must learn to manage our emotional motivations. Doing so helps us to thrive in the workplace as we create a lasting legacy.

Each of these seasons helps us to develop the different facets of our professional identity. These distinct environments create the learning platforms that we use to cultivate our best behaviors so that we can inspire others to reach for their best. Once again, the ultimate purpose of our legacy-making efforts is to inspire others to engage in their own legacy-making efforts. This is how we create a legacy that endures beyond the long winter. We must always remember that carrying others into their legacy is not our job. Instead, we must become comfortable with using the seasons of leadership to lead the way so that they may benefit too.

As we lead with our legacy in mind, our responsibility as a leader is transformed, and we must be constantly focused on learning. Each season of leadership is founded on a bed of self-discovery. It is only when we gain an understanding of how we affect those who share the work experience with us, and how their contributions affect us, that it becomes possible for us to grow into our authentic legacy.

The first step is to realize that every action we take, no matter how small, will ultimately affect the organizations, teams, and people that we work with in some way. Those around us will see every action of ours as either positive or negative, and we must become accountable to our stakeholders for this impact because it will influence the environmental conditions under which they must work.

In essence, the seasons of leadership provide us with the learning opportunities that help us meet our overall developmental objectives. The purpose of the environment is to set the boundaries where we can gain experience. Our struggle is to learn through trial and adversity, which expose us to different situations that become the catalysts for our development. As we do so, we must remember that learning never occurs until we find meaning in the experience. The environmental forces and patterns by themselves can never inspire meaning, and that is why we must always consider the nurturing impact of our journey through the legacy arcs as we seek to understand our environmental circumstances. Our intelligence increases as we apply what we learn in the world around us. The seasons of leadership provide the field for this application. Together, they represent the total work experience, which includes our impact on others.

Our learning is cyclical, which means that we will always be faced with new, but familiar seasons of growth related to our opportunities to follow, lead, and serve. Sometimes it will seem as if we are running through independent cycles, and other times it may feel as if there are concurrent cycles that give us the opportunity to grow and develop simultaneously. Remember, the environment is beyond your control. The only thing you can control is your response to the season in which you find yourself. To fully benefit from these experiences, you must be willing to reflect, to plan, and to make meaning out of the way you use your time. Essentially, each season requires you to use your time wisely.

In Chapter 21, we examine the fundamentals of using time wisely and the impact of our time management skills on our legacy-making efforts. Dr. Marilyn Daudelin, an American author and consultant, believes that reflection is one of the most important actions that leads us through our legacy-making efforts. She said, "Reflection is the process of stepping back from an experience to ponder, carefully and persistently, its meaning to the self through the development of inferences; learning is the creation of meaning from past or current events that serves as a guide for future behavior." The meaning that we make and wish to make helps us to live out our legacy by using our time wisely.

The seasons of leadership not only teach us how to draw meaning from our work experiences, but also teach us much about the legacy-making process.

As we follow, lead, and serve others, we become better acquainted with what we want our legacy to be. These environments become the boundaries for our actions and provide us with opportunities to grow. At times, we may see these boundaries as limits, which can cause us to push against them in nonproductive ways.

The British poet Arthur William Edgar O'Shaughnessy reminds us, "We are the music-makers, and we are the dreamers of dreams." Let these beautiful lines be a constant reminder to us that legacy making is an invitation for us to understand the boundaries so that we can use them for our own benefit. The seasons of leadership belong to us.

Chapter 18

The Season of Following

If I had to reduce the responsibilities of a good follower to a single rule, it would be to speak truth to power.

—WARREN BENNIS

When you were growing up, I doubt that there was ever a time when your mother said to you as you walked out the door, "Be a follower!" In fact, all of us were admonished to be leaders, which meant that every one of us was socialized to believe that being a follower is an undesirable role. Is it any wonder, then, that followership is the harshest of all the legacy environments? We simply don't like being number two.

When we enter the workforce, this belief confuses us because we quickly realize that there are more follower positions than there are leadership roles. We were taught to believe that we were born to be leaders, but as we begin our work experience, we find ourselves occupying some of the least desirable roles and following some of the worst leaders. Eventually, we even realize that no matter how high up we go in the organization, we will always be a follower. There is no escaping the fact that everyone has a boss. This is true of every work-related role.

Because we see following as a "less than" role, we are rarely, if ever, trained in how to be a follower. For this reason, developing the skills of followership can be very difficult, but we must learn to see this as a critical part of our legacy-making efforts. Two of the biggest challenges we face when we find ourselves in the role of follower are learning how to contribute our strengths effectively and learning how to influence the decision makers who either formally supervise us or work across from us in the organization. Very few of us know how to do this, so most of us struggle as we work to find the comfort and power in our various small "l" leadership roles.

We experience this challenge because we have been taught to falsely believe that followers are supposed to be quiet, keep their heads down, and do whatever the Leader commands. The word *subordinate* is often used as a synonym for a follower in the workplace, and this leads us to believe that when we are in the follower role, we lack power, authority, and influence. To be an effective follower, we must learn to see beyond these false assumptions.

In the workplace, a follower must realize that he or she is someone who is authorized to act in accordance with the policies and guidelines of the organization. An effective follower is actively engaged in the efforts that are required to accomplish the company's work. An effective follower must also thoughtfully support the agenda set forth by the leader. This means that the follower is willing to raise his or her voice in opposition when needed. My favorite word to describe the act of following is *go*. This is because followers are actively engaged in implementing the strategy. As followers, we must be ready to go when the next steps come into focus. We see the details better when we are in the follower role, and so we must be willing to report back to those who are more concerned with the big picture. When they get these details, they are more effective in their post.

I am often hired by very large organizations to facilitate the development of their leadership pipeline. These programs are usually branded as high-potential or emerging leader initiatives. As a result, there are many people who are willing to participate in them without receiving additional pay for their time and energy. Imagine what would happen to the participation in these initiatives if these programs were called "followership" initiatives. Do you think anybody would want to be involved?

Lauren's Leadership Story

I met Lauren through some work that I did for a medium-size manufacturing company. She was the president's assistant, and I frequently worked with her to coordinate my calendar with the busy schedules of the senior leadership team. It was easy to be impressed with her efficiency, and I actually enjoyed working with her more than I did with her boss.

Lauren attended all the senior leadership planning meetings. She was not an official member of the team, but she participated in all their interactions. Her primary role was to take the minutes of the meeting and to follow up on the assignments that were made. Most of the time, she sat as a silent observer; her presence was hardly even noticed.

During the course of her normal workday, she connected with many of the organization's other leaders, and she knew many of the frontline workers personally. These relationships were developed through her efforts to support the president. He enjoyed recognizing the individual accomplishments of the employees and the special occasions that they were celebrating. Lauren worked hard to discover successes that would otherwise be missed at the senior leader level, and she was amazing at remembering birthdays, anniversaries, graduations, weddings, and promotions. I think she knew something personal about each one of the 350 employees that worked for the company. Although she did not have a formal leadership title and worked only in a supportive role, Lauren was a leader in the organization, and she was able to see and understand information that was often withheld from the senior leadership team.

In one of the leadership meetings that I attended, the team was discussing an urgent decision that was unrelated to my work. I sat patiently while the debate raged. To be honest, the topic was not that interesting to me, and so I was thinking about some other things. I am not sure what provoked this or how it happened, but suddenly I heard Lauren's voice rise above the din of the conversation. It was clear that she was very concerned about what was being discussed. She did not apologize or excuse herself in any way for entering the fray. She spoke confidently and began to point out something that the team had missed. Unfortunately, some of the team members became defensive and immediately challenged her point of view in a way that actually felt as if they were trying to minimize her opinions so that they could render them irrelevant. Naturally, this brought me back to full consciousness, and I was now very interested in watching the group dynamics on display.

Lauren did not back down. She continued to share her insights despite the many attempts by these leaders to dismiss them. Five of the eight team members openly belittled her, but she held her ground with amazing poise.

After what seemed like a long battle, the president finally spoke. His first words demonstrated why he was the leader. Instead of expressing his own opinion, he turned to the two members of the team who had so far been silent and asked them for their input. With some caution, they both expressed a desire to learn more about what Lauren was trying to say. Instead of pushing back, they began to ask some intelligent questions that they had formed while they were listening to the debate. The answers to those questions began to influence the other team members. Before the meeting was over, a decision that included the information that Lauren had provided, and that was very different from what had originally been intended, was made.

I wish I could say that the five dissenting team members had fully embraced the decision that the team made, but in fact, most of them still felt that Lauren's feedback was inconsequential. They had merely agreed to support the decision while they were in the meeting, and I discovered in subsequent interviews that they did not believe that it would lead to a successful outcome.

The dispute was over the handling of an upcoming meeting with a group of disgruntled employees who were unsatisfied with a challenging process that they felt was making the work conditions for those working on a particular project quite miserable. The leadership team had approved this process because its members had deemed it necessary to control the costs of a tightly bid contract. They wanted to simply impose the unsatisfactory working conditions in the interests of making a profit and were unwilling to hear suggestions from the workers. It was a small company, and the leaders were used to getting their own way. Lauren argued that there was some merit in the workers' complaints, and that it was in the company's best interests to listen to them and see if there was a way to make some positive changes. She had already spoken with many of the workers, and she believed that they had a solution that would both improve the working conditions and increase the profit. She knew that the workers understood the workflow better than the leaders did, and she wanted the leaders to see the situation through the workers' eyes. She knew that this would help them make a more informed decision, even if they decided to keep things the way they were.

A meeting was scheduled with those who were engaged in this particular project, and Mike, one of the team members who had been silent during the fiery debate, was selected to facilitate the conversation. I was asked to help him prepare for the meeting and to attend it as an observer. The other members of the team were also invited to participate as observers. We wanted them to be eyewitnesses to the proceedings, but we cautioned them not to engage in the dialogue. As we prepared for the meeting, we encouraged the workers to also prepare. We asked them to make a presentation that did more than just complain about the unfavorable work conditions. We wanted them to propose alternative solutions and end with a recommendation for how they thought we might succeed in improving the conditions while staying within the confines of the tight budget.

The meeting was a huge success. Even the most skeptical team members came away believing that a better process was possible. No decision was made during the meeting, but Mike promised that the senior leadership team would review the recommendations and return with a decision before the end of the week.

A couple of days later, we reconvened the senior leadership team to finalize a decision. I was amazed by how many opinions had changed and the genuine willingness to make a new decision. The controller had done her homework, and, although she had originally been one of the most avid critics of any new plan, she was very pleased to affirm that one of the strategies recommended by the workforce would actually generate significant savings for the company. This time a unanimously supportive agreement was reached, and Mike went back and green-lighted the new process to the workforce. It is interesting to note that Lauren never said a word in the second meeting; she simply did her job and silently observed the progress that was being made.

This effort created an amazing amount of goodwill between the workforce and the leadership team. Several of the individuals who spoke during the presentation became known by the senior leadership and were frequently asked to help with other decisions. Other "problem" workers were pacified and willingly became owners of the new process.

Key Leadership Lessons

This interaction helped me to clarify a few important characteristics that distinguish good followers from bad ones.

First, each of us must be disciplined enough to lead our own actions. Sometimes when we are in the role of follower, we erroneously believe that we are expected to do nothing until we are instructed to do something. Following is an active process that requires us to use our strengths to support the work in front of us. The best followers are willing to magnify their efforts by lending all of their resources to the success of the project.

Second, effective followers are committed to the purposes of the organization. They understand that their own thoughts and ideas will not always be used in making decisions, but they are willing to share them anyway. They work for a shared success and understand that the collective successes will be more powerful than whatever they might accomplish on their own.

Third, they are willing to invest in building relationships at all levels. They recognize the strengths of their peers, and they look for ways to collaborate effectively on shared work projects and seek to contribute positively when asked about areas that are outside their scope of concern. When they are assigned as managers, they seek the honest feedback of those who report directly to them. The nature of this reporting relationship is clearly understood, and they make sure that their direct reports feel valued. They understand how to influence those who are higher up in the organization. They respect the position, while getting to know the person who is charged with leading. The way they manage these relationships helps them to be constantly contributing to the success of their enterprise. Their voice is respected and heard when it comes time to make new decisions. When new opportunities emerge, they are the first to be asked to help.

The confidence gained through these three actions helps the follower to be courageous, honest, credible, enthusiastic, and self-reliant. These qualities help the effective follower to calmly and openly speak the truth, even in the face of condescending voices. I will always remember the vision of Lauren holding her ground and refusing to give in to the pressure of those who were supposed to be leading. Her willingness to stick with it gave the organization the opportunity to create something much more than a mere concession to pacify a murmuring workforce. She initiated a culture shift that continues to influence her organization to this day. She has since retired, but the legacy that she built as a follower is still felt. The input of the workforce is now sought before any important decisions are made, and the company continues to enjoy success despite its journey through rugged economic times.

It may be true that followership is the harshest of all legacy environments, but we are the ones who choose how we survive or thrive in it. Some people will choose to be cynical, critical, apathetic, and alienated, while others will choose to be enthusiastic, energetic, self-reliant, and purpose-driven. We will witness various levels of growth taking place in this environment, but they will be very different, and so will the quality of the followers' life, work, and legacy experiences.

I saw a sign once on the wall of a military facility in Venezuela. Loosely translated, it read, "You will lead, so learn how to follow." I think about that sign often and wonder why organizations continue to spend so much on leadership development initiatives that rarely live up to their promise, then wonder again why few, if any, resources are ever invested in teaching people how to be effective followers.

The principles of followership, and how individual contributors apply these principles in the work setting, have a significant impact on the success of an organization. Too often we are concerned with one of two questions: "Who is the leader?" and "What must I do to become the leader?" The answers to these two questions do very little to help us establish our legacy.

May I suggest a couple of new questions? Rather than thinking about who is the leader, please direct your attention to the following two questions: "When should I lead?" and "When should I follow?" These questions keep us focused on being an effective leader and follower, and have very little to do with title or position. They are simple reminders that we should use our strengths to make things better in our sphere of influence, the only environment that really matters.

Finally, please erase all fear or concern about being a follower. My roles are always supporting roles, and I usually feel extremely satisfied with the results that we are able to achieve together. Being a follower does not mean that I am not a leader. It simply means that I know when and how to lead effectively from the supporting position. You are never expected to follow blindly. Your leaders want you to think for yourself. They want you to raise issues and concerns. They want you to utilize your positive energy to actively engage in your work. Once they see you in action, you will be given many opportunities to contribute and to share your voice. Remember, there is always somebody who will be following your next step. Your job as a small "l" leader is to show that person how it is done.

Chapter 19

The Season of Leading

Leadership is not magnetic personality—that can just as
well be a glib tongue. It is not "making friends and influencing people"—that is flattery.

Leadership is lifting a person's vision to higher sights,
the raising of a person's performance to a higher standard,
the building of a personality beyond its normal limitations.

—PETER F. DRUCKER

One of the hardest things for those of us who work in the field of
leadership development to accept is this: the results of our efforts
are difficult to define and largely seen as ineffective.

In this year alone, billions of dollars will be invested globally in leadership development strategies. With so much being spent, organizations
have a right to expect significant results. Sadly, many of these initiatives
will fail to achieve their purpose. These are just some of the things we
are finding as we honestly seek to assess the return on these investments.

When we ask followers to anonymously rate the effectiveness of their direct leader, they routinely report it to be between 40 and 50 percent below their expectations. When the same group is asked to rank the most senior leaders in their organization, we find that most of them are rated at or below the twenty-fifth percentile, meaning that the workers think that the efforts of their most senior leaders are bested by 75 percent of all other leaders who are working in other organizations.

Other findings indicate that we are experiencing a significant responsibility shift. Whereas leaders were once respected and thought to be the source of inspiration and answers to problems, many of them are now seen as the villains. Blaming the current leader or the former leader seems to be one of today's most frequently played strategies. Things are always the leader's fault, and the leader is part of the 1 percent that is keeping the 99 percent down.

On the corporate level, we now see a number of very disturbing countertrends as many organizations continue to restructure their workforce in hopes of reducing their fixed costs. The resulting low employment numbers seem to be the new normal, as we find no evidence of increased hiring, even after these companies find their way back to profitability. The mid-level leader is rapidly becoming a position of the past. Instead, we are seeing countless corporations adopting a flat structure, relying more and more on self-directed teams to manage their affairs.

This stormy environment for leaders continues to affect those who would be the leaders of the future. Many of them, having witnessed the nightly televised attacks on our corporate, political, religious, athletic, and celebrity leaders, are deciding that it just isn't worth it and that it might be too dangerous to be a leader. They definitely see it as a social disadvantage to be one of the leaders of the future. Instead of standing up and seeking opportunities to lead, many people are hunkering down and staying out of the limelight.

A recent study by the Zeno Group found that only 15 percent of women between the ages of 21 and 33 feel the desire to become employee number one in a "large or prominent organization." They report that this lack of desire isn't because they don't want success; it's because they just don't think it's worth the price.

All of these variables add up to a couple of stunning findings. First, we have fewer people than ever who want to lead. Second, we have fewer people than ever who are prepared to lead.

There is definitely a dearth of leaders, and the season of leadership is increasingly coming to be seen as a difficult legacy-defining environment. Much of this is because the power and the authority of Leadership roles have been abused. The selfish question "What's in it for me?" has been used by too many people as a guide for gaining leadership influence. The way out is to stop worrying about what we will get, and to start focusing on what we can give in order to influence others through our leadership efforts.

Dale's Leadership Story

When I first met Dale, he escorted me down a long, dark corridor of his office building that separated him from the other employees of his company. We then entered a heavily secured private office space that was rarely seen by others. When I asked him why he had taken such measures to separate himself from his team members, he said, "I don't want them knowing what I am doing."

He had hired me because his leadership flaws had become fatal. Despite his willingness to compensate his employees better than any of his competitors, he was finding it more and more difficult to recruit the people he needed. In addition to this challenge, he was becoming alarmingly suspicious of those who were working for him, and he admitted that he no longer trusted any of them. Dale had a problem, and it was even affecting his relationships with his friends and family. He had once been a prominent community leader, but his behavior had made it necessary for the organizations he served as a volunteer to strip him of his responsibilities.

I accepted the opportunity to work with Dale on the condition that he would do his best to reverse this terrible course. He agreed, but this proved to be very difficult for him to accept. He was extremely paranoid and was unwilling to take responsibility for his abusive behavior. He was always blaming somebody else and trying to convince me that he was right. Vengeance was constantly on his mind, and he spent much of his day figuring out how he was going to get those who had wronged him fired. No matter how hard I tried, I couldn't get him to see how this was affecting his success and his productivity.

We had one shining moment that made me believe for a while that he would take the necessary steps to rehabilitate his tarnished reputation. While we were reviewing his 360-degree feedback, he suddenly saw his own impact, and he knew that he needed to make changes.

I was very happy to see this, and even happier to see him begin at home. He was in trouble with his wife and his children. The gap between them was widening. He stepped up and began to make significant strides at home. I was very satisfied with this progress, but dismayed that he was unwilling to or incapable of making the same kind of effort at work.

Our efforts to right these recurring wrongs became a frequent source of frustration for him. Eventually, he aimed his abusive behavior at me. Reluctantly, I discontinued our relationship. No progress was being made, and I could no longer support him in the way that he needed to be supported.

My experience with Dale continues to be one of my biggest failures as a personal and executive coach. I am sharing it with you because it demonstrates some of the challenges that leadership development professionals face. Not all of our stories have happy endings. This is because our clients are not always willing to work as hard as we are at helping them get better. We can see their potential better, so we reach for it with more energy. This is actually the worst thing we can do. A leader's legacy is a personal choice. It cannot be chosen by anyone else.

Dale is leaving a legacy, and it is a negative one. I have lost track of him, so I hold out for the possibility that he has somehow righted his ship. If he did, I know that this was able to happen only because he was eventually able to disconnect from his fears and connect to his authentic yearnings to be valuable to others. He really did want to be respected and liked by those around him, but he was afraid that they wouldn't do that, and so he continually sabotaged his own efforts.

Naturally, there are many lessons to be learned from this experience. The first learning that I would like to point out is that we must continually be evaluating our own leadership efforts. This means that we must ask ourselves difficult questions so that we can grow in the ways that we need to grow if we are to become better leaders.

I am particularly fond of beginning with a rather sobering question: "What am I doing that is worthy of being followed?" This question helps us to train the focus of our leadership efforts on where it was always meant to be: how our impact is being felt by those that we lead. Sometimes we make things of a personal nature impersonal so that we can escape the growth that we need to experience. We want to grow, but the difficulty is often too much for us to handle, so we ask questions like "What is a good leader?" or "Who is a good leader?" These questions represent the baby steps that we need to take in order to put aside our selfish desires. When we are ready and willing to supercharge our efforts, then we must deepen the inward and personal nature of our questions. Try asking yourself the following as you consider your leadership and legacy desires: "Who is following me, and what am I doing to make things better for them?"

Those of us who are serious about increasing our leadership impact understand that we must eventually learn how to lead others to the next level. We can do that only when we are willing to transform our leadership platform from a concern for self into a total concern for the welfare of those we lead.

There are numerous actions and behaviors that affect your ability to lead others in your formal and informal work-related roles. The good news is that you really have to master only one or two of them to be seen by others as an effective leader. This is true because each real leadership behavior requires us to let go of some of our most significant selfish flaws. I have selected four legacy-building behaviors that model some of the most critical things you can do while you find yourself enjoying the season of leadership.

First, it is extremely important for leaders to create transparency. This means that you bring your agenda as a leader into the open. Too often, we try to hide our leadership agenda, believing that if we bring it into the open, it will be either co-opted or rejected. The biggest complaint of most followers is that their leader doesn't trust them. When we probe why they feel this way, we discover that it is because the leader will not communicate a clear and precise agenda.

A leader must be honest enough to tell the truth and share the details in a way that gives those that follow the opportunity to verify whether the vision is real and then personally choose to follow it. Transparent leaders do this by disclosing, revealing, discussing, and clarifying expectations. They use simple language and are careful to call things what they are, without any attempt to cover up the flaws. This demonstrates their integrity and provides the opportunity to operate in a way that communicates: "What you see here is what you get. You can trust my vision because I am telling you what I am going to do, and I am doing what I said I was going to do."

The transparent leader does not step away from difficult conversations. Instead, she leans into them with a willingness to develop higher levels of conflict competence. This allows her to confront the issues while respecting those who are willing to support the vision.

As a transparent leader, you must be willing to keep all the commitments you make. They must be the symbol of your honor. In order to keep all the commitments you make, you must learn how to say no gracefully. This demonstrates your willingness to lead, without turning your legacy into a popularity contest. The popular choices are not always the right choices, and leaders must be willing to lose popularity in exchange for credibility.

The second behavior that helps us enjoy the season of leadership is a willingness to constantly reach for the next level. Leaders must be committed to continuous improvement. Only those who are willing to be lifelong learners can create a meaningful legacy.

Information is what accelerates learning. When we truly commit ourselves to becoming better leaders, then we open ourselves up to the opinions of others. We should do very little to debate the opinions of our followers. Instead, we should accept them for what they are: a representation of what somebody else is experiencing when he or she follows our lead. Feedback is definitely a gift. We value that gift by discovering ways in which we can honor the suggestions we receive.

Responding to feedback requires us to let go of our ego. This demonstrates personal humility, which paves the way for more honest and targeted suggestions in the future. When those who follow us believe that we are truly willing to honestly consider their hopeful suggestions for our improvement, they become more willing to offer us helpful suggestions and allow us the opportunity to respond. We don't have to honor every bit of feedback we receive by making a new decision. Doing so would drive most of our stakeholders batty, and they wouldn't really know what we stand for. The best way to honor these suggestions is to be grateful for them and to follow up with others on the actions that we decide to take. This gives them a chance to help us in our efforts to be accountable for what we say we are going to do, and it demonstrates that we are unwilling to allow our personal pride to get in the way of our doing the right thing. When we take responsibility for our results, even when things turn out wrong, our legacy is strengthened, and we are respected for all that we do and trusted to do the right thing.

Another key behavior in the season of leadership is knowing when and how to inspire and empower others. To do this effectively, we must constantly be doing our best to recognize the strengths of others, but simply recognizing them is not enough. We must also be willing to speak encouraging words that lift others up to new levels. Most of the time, the little successes in the workplace seem to go unnoticed. The leader should not only see the little things, but comment kindly when he or she sees them. Remember not to wait too long, because when time passes, the little things lose their relevance.

One of the keys to inspiring others is the consistent modeling of a spirit of optimism. Be positive! This doesn't mean being foolishly or falsely optimistic. You can begin by looking around, noticing what is going right, and then commenting on that.

A question that I ask one of my clients every day is: "How many angry, destructive, or judgmental comments did you make today?" This reminds him to treat people in a kindly way, to always speak about those who are absent as if they were present, and to genuinely care for others. It also helps him to strengthen the levels of trust that he has with others because they know that they can count on him to be their friend even when they are not around.

The final key behavior that helps us through the season of leadership is to invite others to participate. For some reason, there are many people who sit on the sidelines until they are asked to get involved. Please remember the story of Mike and Lauren in Chapter 18. They really needed to be provoked and invited to participate, but when they did, it made a huge difference.

For some reason, followers think that they must be invited to comment or act. The leadership models of the past sometimes reinforced this poor model. Peter Drucker once said that the "leader of the past knew how to tell" people what to do, "the leader of the future will know how to ask." When we ask people to share their opinion, lead a project, share their strength, and be involved, we give them permission to soar in ascending spirals.

This behavior really requires us to use our active listening and hearing skills. When we do that, we become aware of how each person can contribute, and then we can honor this awareness by asking each of them to be involved.

As you consider these four opportunities to increase your leadership footprint, please take a moment to think about the question I asked you earlier in this chapter:

"What am I doing that is worthy of being followed?"

Now let me ask you the same question in a different way:

"What makes you a great leader?"

As you ponder these two questions, make sure to capture the thoughts that enter your mind. They will guide you to the behaviors that you are already doing best. May I suggest that instead of working on something that you are struggling to do, you focus your energy on doing more of what you are already doing pretty well? There is room for you to improve. Don't be afraid to do it.

Key Leadership Lessons

Naturally, it is my hope that as you read this book, you will experience several personal "aha" moments. Hopefully, some of your previous experiences with others may have begun to make a little more sense. I even hope that you are able to uncover some of the blind spots that prevent you from creating your legacy.

In every single interaction, I have noticed that most leaders are comfortable keeping themselves blind to their blind spots. Some of their blind spots really are just that: the leader cannot see them, so he or she really can't do anything about them. The sad part is that some people are content with doing nothing to discover the blind spots that they have.

Even sadder is the fact that there are some people who are aware of their blind spots, and yet go around foolishly believing that they can keep them hidden from others. This is a false hope. Those around you can see your weaknesses, and they are patiently hoping for you to do something about them.

The best leaders are constantly getting the external feedback that they need in order to learn and grow. They don't resist the idea of getting feedback; instead, they seek it out. Getting feedback actually gets harder as you climb up the corporate ladder. If you really want it, then you must learn to ask for it authentically. This means that you will have to create a safe environment in which to do so.

Please realize that people will be more open to giving you honest feedback if you give them the opportunity to do so anonymously. This is because they really do want to help you, and they really don't want to hurt you. The anonymous format gives them the chance to focus on the behavior and not the person. You must do your best to create a safe zone in which feedback can be given.

Feedback is important, but feedforward is essential. Feedforward is a positive, future-focused personal development process that takes the judgment and critical sting out of helping someone get better. It shifts the focus from rehashing the mistakes of the past to concentrating on the promises of the future. We cannot change the past, but we can create the future. Because feedforward is future-focused, it is an excellent tool to use when creating your legacy.

The feedforward process does not eliminate the need for feedback. Instead, it creates an additional tool for you to use while leveraging the perspectives of others, thereby accelerating your growth.

Some people will never get comfortable enough to give their leader feedback. They see it as just too big a risk for their career. Yet most people, when invited, are more than willing to share ideas about how somebody can get better in the future. To be clear, feedforward is the process of gaining positive suggestions from others that are pertinent to improving your personal behavior. Feedforward is always forward-looking, positive in nature, focused on potential, and evocative of a desire to grow.

Your success in leveraging the perceptions of others depends entirely upon your ability to involve your stakeholders in the feedforward process. A stakeholder is a person who is in a position to witness and evaluate your behavior. Often, stakeholders are directly affected by the impact of the behavior that you wish to grow.

Think about this for a moment. Which scenario creates a stronger perception in others that your behavior is changing—allowing them to give you feedback, or implementing a positive, forward-looking suggestion that they gave you through feedforward? The answer is quite obvious. Your stakeholders feel validated when you implement one of their suggestions. This evokes an even greater desire on their part to help you in the future.

The Feedforward Method

Feedforward is an extremely useful tool for us to use as we create our legacy. Because this idea might be new to many of you, I wish to share a few tips before we move on to the next chapter. I learned these tips from my work with Marshall Goldsmith. Marshall is known as one of the originators of this concept.

First, be sure to include as many stakeholders as possible in the process, but invite only those who are genuinely committed to helping you. You do not need to have the process tainted by negative suggestions from people who have no interest in helping you grow.

Second, make sure to keep the process positive. If you are feeling defensive, then wait for a better time to be involved.

Third, make sure you develop some sort of reminder system to ensure your consistency in following up with your stakeholders. In order to get timely suggestions, you must follow up regularly.

Fourth, be careful not to grade the ideas you receive from others, and make sure to thank each stakeholder for his or her willingness to help you get better. You are not thanking your stakeholders for their suggestions; you are thanking them for helping you.

Fifth, make sure that you keep the process as informal as possible. You do not need to schedule your stakeholder moments; just stop by, call them up, or send an e-mail.

Sixth, it is very important that you clearly define the help you wish to receive. You cannot expect to get good feedforward if your request is vague.

Seventh, keep the conversations very simple: "Bob, I am working on becoming better at (fill in the blank). Can you give me some positive, forward-looking suggestions on how I can accelerate my progress?

Finally, accept what you hear as being true from your stakeholder's perspective. Don't ever debate it. Remember, you do not have to implement every suggestion to be successful. Debating a suggestion will make it feel like feedback, and will reduce your chances of getting feedforward in the future. Just say, "Thank you."

As you ask for feedforward, you may hear two statements that are not very helpful:

You are already doing a great job.
I can't think of anything to tell you.

When you hear these statements, just ask your stakeholder to think about somebody he or she knows who does what you are trying to do in a very effective way. Then ask your stakeholder to tell you what that person does to be so effective.

If your stakeholders are still unable to give you any suggestions, remind them that you will be working on this behavior for a while and ask them to think about ways in which you can improve. Then tell them that you will follow up with them later. Make sure you set a date in your own calendar to follow up, and then make sure you do it.

Don't forget, your ability to create your best leadership legacy is directly correlated with the amount of time you spend engaging your stakeholders.

I always feel the urge to remind you that leadership is about making things better. If this is the only thing you hear, then I consider my purposes for writing this book to have been met. You are the leader. Go out and make things better.

Chapter 20

The Season of Serving

The best way to find yourself is to lose yourself in the service of others.

—Mahatma Gandhi

Let's face it, creating a legacy is meaningless if we do not know why we are doing it. If we really expect our leadership efforts to matter, then we must learn to connect the value of our work experiences with something more meaningful than profit margins and position power. We need to build a living balance sheet that is constantly uniting us with something that is bigger than ourselves. These connections bring us into alignment with the purposes that will sustain us in the adventures of trading time for money. Without the right purpose, we can't even hang on, let alone cross the finish line of a productive and meaningful career.

One purpose that we must honor as we reach for our legacy is that of using the gifts and talents that we develop to bless and nourish the lives of others. A legacy must never be a selfish pursuit, or else our enlightened moments will certainly be overcome by darkness.

The road to a legacy is never traveled alone. If we truly want to enjoy what we are gaining, then we must be willing to share what we have with those around us. Those who travel this road silently by themselves stumble and fall along the way, making it impossible for them to ever reach their desired destination. Their legacy fades quickly. Consequently, they never realize their true potential. They feel the stress, the pain, and the sorrow of life, instead of the beauty, the joy, and the happiness that is waiting for all who learn to serve others.

I was once closely associated with a very successful man. His many achievements were the emblems of his success. He enjoyed the finer things in life and traveled the world in first-class cabins.

One day, we were having a conversation. My wife and I had recently moved into a new home in a distant town, resulting in a pretty major commute to the office. I told him that I was worried about the miles I was putting on my car. He said that he was worried about the miles that I was putting on myself.

Our new home was beautiful, and we were living in a wonderful area. For the first time in our marriage, we felt as if we belonged to a community. We were involved, and there were many opportunities for us to love and serve others. I considered his concern, and then I told him that we were much happier living in this faraway town. He then said something that completely surprised me. He said, "I wouldn't know anything about that. I have never been happy."

Here was a man who had the best of everything. He was a successful businessman. He made a lot of money, yet he said that he had never been happy. I am convinced that he was unhappy because he had time only to pursue his own self-interests. Since that time, I have met many other successful people who feel the same way. It is not really that they are unhappy; they just know that they are missing something. They know that there is something more. They have the dream car, the dream house, and the dream life, but they are often longing for something more. They worry about the legacy that they are creating, and they silently wonder, "Is this really all there is?"

Of course there is something more, but we cannot find what we are naturally looking for by working harder to achieve more. Our achievements will never fill us up. They can only be, and were always only meant to be, a part of what it takes to fill us up. They make up many of the foundational experiences that set the tone for our legacy-making efforts, but they can take us only so far.

Giving Back

Sometimes we forget that we live in abundance. We hold on to what we have with clenched fists instead of open hands. Our attention is so firmly fixed on achieving more that we forget to look around us to discover how we can create more meaning by serving others.

Meaningful experiences come to us more abundantly when we serve and help others. We cannot enjoy our legacy by ourselves. When the fruits of our work experience are ready to be harvested, we must share them with those around us, or else they will rot and decay.

It is during the season of service that we learn the purpose of our successes and the secret to leading with our legacy in mind. Our ability to grow and to develop is dependent upon our willingness to share our successes with others. Sadly, there is usually some sort of politically motivated action that is designed to force us to share our resources with others. I say that this is sad because when we are compelled to do this, we lose the beautiful outcomes that are so closely associated with voluntarily serving others. We must not wait to be compelled to give in meaningful ways. When we are compelled, our freedom is violated, and we lose the meaning that comes from happily giving from our own heart.

Our successes are to be shared via acts of free will. This is the only way that we can truly make them meaningful. Living up to our legacy requires us to be consistently thinking and acting about ways in which we can create opportunities for others to also live up to their own legacy. We will not enjoy our successes until we see that they are given to us so that we can help others succeed.

Too many of us forget that abundance is a quality and not a quantity. It is measured by the way we feel in our heart and the simple actions that we take to make things around us better. For some reason, we think that since we do not have Bill Gates's money, we can't be a servant or a philanthropist. It doesn't take money to do this; it takes a willing heart.

I want to share three brief examples of how we can be philanthropists and servants on a budget. They powerfully illustrate the only required ingredient: love of others.

Jeffery: Mentoring

I met Jeffery when he was nearly 60 years old. He had enjoyed many successes and faced many trials over the course of his lifetime. When we met, he was facing some pretty significant challenges. Despite these challenges, he was always willing to help others. His cash flow was tight, and for the first time in a long time he was struggling to meet his own needs. However, this never prevented him from sharing what he did have with others. Sometimes he contributed some of his scarce physical resources to those who had less than he did, and he was always giving of his time.

As we worked together to define and establish his legacy, he became acquainted with some of my children and began to feel a special connection with my son Jacob, who was just starting his career and family life.

Jeffery was just righting his own ship. He could have been focused on his own challenges, but that was not his way of being. He held a bright vision of the future, and he was willing to share his struggles and his triumphs with Jacob, so he offered himself as a mentor. His frequent contact with Jacob made him feel useful, and this service was something that Jacob enjoyed very much. They became accountability partners, thinking partners, and supporting partners. Their relationship was mutually beneficial. They helped each other grow, and now Jeffery's legacy will live on through Jacob's actions. I am certain that Jacob will one day reach out to a much younger man and offer the same kind of help. This is something that he learned from Jeffery.

Jeffery was willing to give back. At 60 years old, he was healthy and wise, and so he shared his wisdom with many others. He understood the power of his legacy, and so he used his work experiences to educate the people he met along the way.

Who in your circle of influence would benefit most from your wisdom and knowledge?

What can you do to mentor that person today?

Tyler: Serving

I met "Tyler Do Good" when we were both speaking at TEDxGreenville in 2010. At the time, he was just 21 years old. Tyler grew up in a wonderful home. Although he was aware of and grateful for his good fortune, he still found himself suffering from depression. As he stared at himself in the mirror one morning in the early spring of 2009, he decided to make a positive change. He immediately began to plan a tour of service. In the summer between his sophomore and junior years in college, he left his home in upstate New York and began a road trip to the Florida Keys. His goal was to help as many people as he could along the way. He drove the back roads. When he saw someone outside, he would pull over, get out of his car, and say, "Hi, my name is Tyler. Can I help you with something?"

Naturally, this action provoked a lot of chaos. Most people wondered if he was trying to steal something from them, but that did not stop him from continuing his quest to serve as many people as he possibly could.

Living out of his car, he committed 115 random acts of service for complete strangers. As he served, he asked the people he met one simple question: "What is one life lesson you have learned?" His service and the answers to this question changed his life. He continues to help out where he can and when he can. He is a model of the beauty that is shining from our young people today. They understand how service forms and shapes a legacy. There are many young people who are finding ways to serve others. Don't be left behind.

Look around and consider these two questions:

What needs are waiting to be met?
What can I do to meet them?

Brad: Service Projects

During the course of writing this book, I became familiar with the work of Brad Jamison. When he was 37 years old, Brad took a break from his award-winning professional career to found Good Citizen, an organization that is dedicated to improving the world through simple acts of service. His vision is to help us all be "good citizens" so that together we can change the world.

Brad realized that he needed to establish credibility so that he could speak authentically about this vision. His first action as the CEO of Good Citizen was to engage in a project that committed him to performing 30 service projects in 30 different organizations over the course of 30 days.

When he had finished the project, he declared, "My life has been transformed! I've moved from feelings of low self-esteem, failure, and anger to great levels of joy, gratitude, clarity, and more. How did I do it? By serving others—something that anyone can do."

Opportunities to serve others are all around us. They stare us in the face, and when we pay attention, we see them. Once we see them, we have a decision to make: we can either meet the need or quietly walk away. It really is our choice, and we *can* make a difference.

Jeffery, Tyler, and Brad represent us all. They feel a desire to serve each day. You and I feel that desire, too. Don't let a busy schedule prevent you from getting involved. If you want to create a legacy, then you must be a creator of circumstances. You can't just go to work and allow it to happen to you.

Norman Cousins, a well-known political journalist and advocate for world peace, once said, "If something comes to life in others because of you, then you have made an approach to immortality."

You and I know this. Will we honor it?

Work is an everyday experience. We get to be with others, whether we like it or not. We don't have to quit our jobs or take a long trip in order to serve others. There are opportunities to serve all around us, right here in our own neighborhoods. Will we find them?

Key Leadership Lessons

These inspiring examples are merely meant to remind us of what is possible. Each day, we can look around us and find a way to give back, to serve others, and to offer help where it is needed. The great work of creating a legacy is an everyday commitment. As we serve others, we engage in the process of discovering who we are. This helps us to become the person we are meant to be and ensures that our legacy will be felt for many years to come.

As our careers become established and stable, the questions that contribute to the construction of our legacy become more obvious.

We think about these questions often, yet for some reason we tell our-selves that we will get to them "some other day."

Unfortunately, "some other day" rarely comes, and "legacy making" continues to be a topic that is only occasionally found in our daily conver-sations. Sadly, for too many people, the supply of tomorrows eventually runs out without their ever having given their legacy the consideration it deserves. Don't be one of them.

Shaping our legacy requires us to serve others. We don't serve them because they are less than we are; we serve them because we want to inspire them to be more than they are. When we do this, our interactions with others are positive. Though many of these experiences will be brief and sometime anonymous, they will touch both others and ourselves in ways that will continually inspire personal growth and development.

This is the general purpose of life and work. We are here to learn and grow through our own experiences. It is easy to be self-centered in this pursuit, but it is only when we extend our strengths outward that we realize that service fills us with a greater sense of joy than we will ever know doing anything else. Service is the most significant contributor to our legacy. It happens in an environment that enriches and accelerates our growth.

I regularly visit with individuals who are nearing the end of their careers. One of the questions I like to ask during my time with these wise individuals is, "What is the most important lesson you have learned from your work experiences?" Their responses to this question are amazingly similar. Here are the five most common answers I hear:

The opportunities we have to contribute matter more than the financial rewards we receive.

Leading without a title or a formal role is often more rewarding than being in charge.

It is awesome to follow a leader who knows where he or she is going
and understands how to make things better.
Service to others is the most satisfying use of my talent and energy.
Working smart is more valuable than working hard. The joy of our
duty is felt most prominently when we share our strengths with
others.

There they are, the secrets to finding joy through your work experiences. Do any of them surprise you? I wonder if we fully appreciate the valuable wisdom that is found in these simple declarations from those who will soon cross the finish line of their career and their life. If we do, we will build our own work experiences around them.

These are the answers, and we have been given permission to use them. If a teacher gave you the answers to an important test, and also gave you permission to use those answers on the test, would you ignore them? Of course not! That would be ridiculous. You would use them to your advantage.

No matter where you are on the arc of your career, today is the best day to study these answers and to begin ordering your work experiences around them. Real opportunities to grow your legacy are waiting for you right now. Don't miss out on any of them because you are so caught up in the busyness of your work, especially the opportunities to serve others. These will give you more energy than anything else you can do.

Before we move on, please take a moment to think about the people in your circle of influence. Consider their successes and their strengths. Now think about how you can serve them.

Write down the names of the people that you will help. Write down how you will help them in the next 30 days.

Now, follow up on these desires and offer your help. Some of these people may think that you are trying to gain some advantage over them, and some may not accept your help. Others may want you to help them in a different way from the way you envisioned. Whatever happens, there is always an opportunity to add value. Just reach out, and you will be leading with your legacy in mind.

Our actions, the way we serve others, and the way we reach for our legacy are the footprints we leave behind for those who follow to examine and celebrate. Be there!

This final thought comes from my friend Jeffery. I use it because it captures a willingness to always be ready to serve others: "I am the one you want to be with if you are ever lost in the wilderness. I will guide you safely out." What a great statement to guide our legacy-making efforts. Be a servant who guides others safely out.

Chapter 21

Using Time Wisely

Time is what we want most, but what we use worst.

—WILLIAM PENN

Simply put, legacy making is nothing more than an exercise in using time wisely. Whether your focus is on the next 525,600 minutes or the rest of the 117,000 hours that you will spend over the course of your career, your legacy requires you to use each moment on purpose.

I confess that I am one of the best time wasters I know. I want the same thing you want. I want to get the most out of my day, but I often fall captive to the noise of the world. Its bright lights and big cities are so attractive that I can easily forget what I want most.

Creative avoidance is nurtured by the hours we spend in front of the boob tube, mindlessly surfing the Internet, compulsively checking our social network interfaces to read friendly but often meaningless messages, and fixing our focus on our smartphones to text without purpose. All of these wonderful experiences suck away so many of our prime legacy-making moments. I do not doubt that these wonderful techno-tools can help us establish our legacy, but most of the time they are our main sources of distraction. We must learn to use them in moderation. Remember that they were invented to reduce our work-related efforts. How is that working out for us?

The next time you are in a business meeting, note how often somebody is either openly or secretly leaving the meeting via some virtual portal. This even happens at the family dinner table. Our legacy is about using our time to make an impact. To do that, we must be present. We can't make things better for those around us if we are mentally in some other world. We must be present.

Because I am such a good time waster, I have spent a lot of time carefully studying what makes us use our time most effectively. I want to understand what it takes, so that I can always use my time wisely. This personal study has had an impact on the way I live, and on my capacity for being with people. One of my clients recently told me that I have figured out a way to drop out of the meaningless so that I can live into the meaningful.

I do not claim to have any special ability. As I said, I struggle with this. In fact, only a few things have changed since the plane ride home from Argentina. That experience helped me to look at time differently. I knew that I would never be able to balance it, so I started looking for ways to use it more effectively. My search led me to some very important realizations. They may seem rather obvious, but I have learned from many personal and vicarious experiences that we do not always understand—or, for that matter, know how to do—the obvious. For this reason, I am sharing these learnings with you now.

I put a great deal of thought into figuring out how to end this book. It has been on my mind since I began to write it. It is not so much that I wanted to say something profound as we say goodbye; I simply wanted to be prepared for this moment.

I realize that this book now becomes a part of my professional legacy, but more than that, I want it to be a tool for you to use in creating your own legacy. I ask you many questions within these pages. My hope is that you will now invest some of your precious time in considering them. I understand the value of time. It is the only nonrenewable resource that we have. We can get more of everything else. Only our time will eventually run out. With that in mind, I wish to share with you some of the lessons I have learned about using time wisely. I have saved the best for last. I know that using our time wisely is the most important ingredient in our legacy-making efforts. These learnings sum up this effort. They bring its purpose to life.

The Role of Purpose

I mention purpose a lot in this book. This is because we cannot build a legacy without a purpose. Time is also best used when it is guided by a purpose.

One of the questions that we most often wonder about is, "What is the purpose of life?" Because we spend so much time of our life at work, we can also ask, "What is the purpose of work?"

It is important for us to realize that there are general purposes and specific purposes. This means that some purposes fit all of us, and others are individual. Therefore, I can give you the general answer to the question, "What is the purpose of life/work?," but I cannot give you the specific answers. Only you can give those responses.

Here it is. The purpose of life and work is to learn and grow through your own experiences. That's it. It's that simple.

The way we use our time, which by the way represents our specific and individual answers to this question, deeply influences our ability to create a legacy. Therefore, the founding action for creating a legacy is discovering and understanding the specific purposes that will guide us along the way. We will not use our time wisely until we connect to these purposes.

What are the specific purposes that guide you? (If you are having trouble answering this question, please remember that a purpose is nothing more than an objective. Your purposes will change as you grow. They come into your mind when you ask, "What do I want now?" Your work in discovering your specific and timely purposes can happen only when you step away and evaluate what you want. Your legacy calls you to take that action.)

Key Indicators

Your next step is to determine how you will measure your success. Please note that this is how you make meaning. Success is simply a construct or an idea that we use to help us feel good about the results that we create. There are a bazillion and one ways to define the successful accomplishment of the same purpose. My way will be different from yours, even when we are reaching for the same purpose. It is important to note this, because we might be working with one another to accomplish the same purpose, but using different measurement tools.

In Chapter 11, we examine the legacy arc that moves us from acceptance to understanding. This arc helps us to appreciate and value the different ways of measuring success, and allows us to see that there are many paths that can lead us to a vibrant legacy.

Acknowledging and defining our individual milestones in advance helps us to always be recalibrating our actions, especially when we begin to drift away from what we say we value most.

Until we establish the milestones that we will use to guide us to our legacy, we will be unable to say whether we are using our time wisely or foolishly wasting it. Our key indicators help us to stay on track. They remind us of the actions and acquisitions that will bring us the most meaning. They keep us going when we get discouraged.

Planning

Time is never wisely used without a plan. After we clearly define our purposes and the key indicators that will mark and measure our success, we are ready to think about the way we will go about living up to it.

Planning is the careful creation of an action before it happens. Creation will always occur in two phases: a mental map, followed by physical action. As we look at the mental map, we are able to examine our decisions, and their resulting impacts, before we make them. While our purposes and our key indicators represent our desires, planning helps us to establish our priorities.

Planning uses our imagination. It helps us to visualize what is most important and creates the energy that we need if we are to become our best. It makes sure that our work experiences are carefully aligned with the actions that will best lead to a legacy. It is probably the most creative exercise that we will ever do. It helps us to stay fresh and connected with what matters most.

We must always be planning on two levels: short term and long term. Long-term planning is at least a weekly activity, and short-term planning is a must as a daily activity. When we plan consistently, we connect to our core values effectively, which then leads us to the next step: setting the right goals.

Goal Setting

We are obsessed with goal setting. We are taught from an early age that goal setting determines success. As a result, we are actually pretty good about setting goals. However, I want you to notice where goal setting appears in this process.

Goal setting is the last step in the process that helps us to use our time wisely. Too many of us make it the first step. Unfortunately, because we are always living at the speed of life, this usually means that we never take the time to connect our goals to our purposes, meaning, or planning efforts. Is it any wonder that we break our New Year's resolutions by January 2, or that many of us go through life feeling as if we are unable to get what we want?

Without proper alignment with our purpose and meaning through careful planning, we are truly just wasting our time. We may feel busy and even successful, because we are in motion, but ultimately our results remind us that we are not getting what we want.

Goal setting is the last step because we cannot know what we want to do until we know who we are and where we want to go. Our direction is defined by our purpose and meaning. Planning helps us to identify our priorities, and goal setting identifies the appropriate actions.

Key Leadership Lessons

This is the simple process that determines our legacy: clarifying our purpose, understanding what brings meaning, planning with our purpose and meaning in mind, and then setting goals that lead us to accomplish our purpose. Not only does this determine our legacy, but it also determines how we use our time. When we follow this simple process, we feel the energy of our legacy propelling us forward.

How are you using your time?
Are you satisfied with your answer to that question?
What adjustments do you need to make?

What is the smallest action that you can take to create the biggest
    impact on your work experience?
Are you willing to take that action today?

Work has always been part of the legacy-making equation. Time represents the framework or the playing field upon which the game is played. You will spend more time at work than anywhere else, and the choices you make in engaging in work experiences will affect your life experiences in significant ways.

You will work at something today, and that work will either add to or subtract from your legacy. You can work to make a living, or you can work to make a legacy. It really is your choice.

What will your legacy be?
Will it be something that you create on purpose?
Will you use your work experiences to make things better?
Will you lead with your legacy in mind?

Hunter Thompson provided us with a wonderful vision of our legacy-making potential when he said, "Life should not be a journey to the grave with the intention of arriving safely in a pretty and well preserved body, but rather to skid in broadside in a cloud of smoke, thoroughly used up, totally worn out, and loudly proclaiming 'Wow! What a Ride!'"

That is what I want to say about my legacy-making efforts, and that is what I want you to say about yours. You are the author and the driver of your experiences. See you on the road!

Recommended Reading

Also by the author:

Andrew L. Thorn, *U-wun-ge-lay-ma: A Guide to Next Level Living* (Apple Valley, CA: Telios Press, 2010).

Also by Marshall Goldsmith, author of the Foreword:

Marshall Goldsmith, *Mojo: How to Get It, How to Keep It, How to Get It Back If You Lose It* (New York: Hyperion, 2009).

Marshall Goldsmith, *What Got You Here Won't Get You There: How Successful People Become Even More Successful* (New York: Hyperion, 2007).

Other recommended titles:

The Arbinger Institute, *Leadership and Self-Deception: Getting Out of the Box* (San Francisco: Berrett-Koehler, 2000).

Craig Hickman, Tom Smith, and Roger Connors, *The Oz Principle: Getting Results Through Individual and Organizational Accountability* (New York: Penguin Group, 2004).

James Kouzes and Barry Posner, *A Leader's Legacy* (San Francisco: Jossey-Bass, 2006).

Richard Leider, *The Power of Purpose: Find Meaning, Live Longer, Better* (San Francisco: Berrett-Koehler, 1997).

Chris Lowney, *Heroic Leadership* (Chicago: Loyola Press, 2003).

C. Otto Scharmer, *Theory U: Leading from the Future as It Emerges* (San Francisco: Berrett-Koehler, 2009).

Robin Sharma, *The Leader Who Had No Title: A Modern Fable on Real Success in Business and in Life* (London: Simon & Schuster, 2010).

Rosamund Stone Zander and Benjamin Zander, *The Art of Possibility: Transforming Personal and Professional Life* (Boston: Harvard Business School Press, 2000).

John Zenger and Joseph Folkman, *The Extraordinary Leader: Turning Good Managers into Great Leaders* (New York: McGraw-Hill, 2002).

Index

About the Author

Dr. Andrew Thorn provides behavioral-based leadership strategies to individuals who are seeking to bring their personal and professional responsibilities into full harmony. His clients achieve more, become more, and experience balanced growth for their own benefit and for the benefit of the people they lead.

His confidential work with senior leaders and C-level executives over the past 25 years helps him establish trust quickly and deeply. He is known for his ability to address difficult conversations without creating conflict. He fosters a strength-based approach and is constantly looking for ways to help people become the best they can be.

He personally guided two of the top 50 business thinkers currently listed on the Thinkers50. His work extends to more than 50 major corporate clients and more than 250 senior leaders from many of the Fortune 500 companies.

A pioneer and leader in the field of work/life focus, Andrew is widely recognized for his breakthrough thinking on how to help people discover their sense of purpose and create greater meaning from their personal and professional experiences.

Dr. Thorn holds a PhD in Consulting Psychology, a master's in Business Administration, and a master's in Personal and Executive Coaching.

He is happily married to Stacy, his wife of 25 years, and they are the parents of seven children. He is active in his church and in his children's lives, while at the same time challenging himself and setting an example by actively living a life of inventure and purpose.

For more information, please visit www.andrewthorn.com.